TESTING EARLY JETS

Testing Early Jets

Compressibility and the Supersonic Era

Roland Beamont

Foreword by Sir Peter Masefield, M.A., C.Eng., FRAeS, Hon.D.Tech.

Airlife
England

Copyright © Roland Beamont, 1990

First published in UK in 1990
by Airlife Publishing Ltd.

British Library Cataloguing in Publication Data
Beamont, Roland *1920–*
    Testing early jets.
    1.   Aeroplanes Test flights
    I.   Title
    629.13453

ISBN 1 85310 158 3

Printed in England

Airlife Publishing Ltd.

101 Longden Road, Shrewsbury, SY3 9EB, England

CHAPTERS

Author's Note

The opinions expressed in the following chapters are the author's and do not necessarily reflect those of any other authority referred to in the text.

Acknowledgements

The author expresses grateful thanks to the many sources of information and assistance received in compiling this book, and in particular to Hr Heinrich Beauvais of the Rechlin Test Centre, 1939-45; Reed Business Publishing for the use of material previously published for the author in *Aeroplane Monthly*; British Aerospace for quotations from Warton flight test reports; Chrys Butcher and the Warton photographic department for their invaluable help; John W. R. Taylor of 'Janes'; Greg Ferguson and Peter Holman of British Aerospace, Kingston and Stevenage; and Arthur Reed; for their great assistance with photographs; Joan Moores for coping once again and so well with the interpretation and typing of the manuscript; the USAF Interceptor Weapons School Magazine; to Floyd McGowin of Chapman, Alabama; to British Airways Concorde Flight; and, as always, to my wife Pat for the vital discipline of her proof-reading and sound advice.

To J. L. 'Jimmy' Dell and, finally, to that most distinguished British total aviation person Sir Peter Masefield, for his generous Foreword.

Dedication

To the engineers who strive for ultimate safety, and to the test pilots who accept the risks to prove it.

Foreword
by Sir Peter Masefield

There are very few of whom it can be said that — within their special field — they have become 'legends in their own lifetime'. One of that rare breed is Roland Beamont — 'Bee' to a legion of friends. His remarkable flying career has, indeed, no parallel.

Now, in this important book, he adds significantly to his attainments by a concise and wide-ranging account of the exploration of the turbulent flying characteristics of aircraft pushed, step-by-step, towards Mach 1, and beyond, through the unknowns of compressibility and the 'uncontrollabilities' that went with them.

This book is important for three special reasons. First, for the facts and the informed comments which it provides on the performance and the handling characteristics of some of the most significant fighter aircraft of the immediate post-War period. Second, because it illuminates more clearly than ever before the problems — and the hazards — which beset the path through the 'thermal thicket' to the smooth uplands enjoyed by latter-day aircraft, which (thanks to their test pilots) have been contrived to be well-mannered at supersonic speeds. And third, because it fills notable gaps in modern technological and aeronautical history.

'Bee' Beamont — with a few of his equally courageous flying colleagues (some of whom, sadly, did not survive) 'rode the storm' through the unexplored perils of the advance to what used to be called 'the sound barrier'. The story of those days, and of the aircraft involved, is an epic chapter of aviation history.

As the book shows, Beamont brought to his flying career exceptional qualities of application, keenness, and skill which were further enhanced as his experience widened and grew.

As a fledgling fighter pilot with No. 87 Squadron, RAF, flying Hawker Hurricanes, he was in France with the Advanced Air Striking Force through those chaotic days of the German onslaught to the Channel ports in May and June of 1940. Thereafter, with the re-formed Squadron operating from Exeter, he fought in the Battle of Britain and in the subsequent fighter sweeps against the Luftwaffe in France.

After a break as a production test pilot with Hawker Aircraft Limited at Langley, he joined No. 56 Fighter Squadron, newly formed with Typhoons. Then, as Commanding Officer of No. 609 Squadron, R.Aux.A.F., he exploited to the full for the first time the Typhoon's devastating ground attack qualities, earning a Bar to his earlier DFC and gaining appointment to the DSO.

Back at Langley briefly, he continued his test-flying career with Hawker, specifically on the formidable new Tempest, and went on to command the first Tempest Wing at Newchurch. From here, three days after D-Day, he recorded a Messerschmitt 109 as the Tempest's first combat victory. To that he added a bag of thirty-two V-1 flying-bombs before the Wing advanced into Europe. Flying from the Netherlands airfield at Volkel on 4 October 1944, he was shot down, captured and spent the remaining months of the war in a prison camp.

With peace, a return home and a Bar to his DSO, he was posted to command the Air Fighting Development Squadron at the Central Fighter Establishment. From there, he came back to test flying with the first of the new generation of jet fighters — the Gloster Meteor and the de Havilland Vampire. Having decided not to take up the offer of a permanent commission with the Royal Air Force, in 1947 he joined instead the English Electric Company at Warton as Chief Test Pilot.

Thus began an epic period in which Beamont not only made a major contribution to the development of the outstandingly successful Canberra jet bomber — including its adoption by the United States Air Force as the B-57 (built under licence by the Glenn Martin Company) — but also, in 1948, was invited to assess the flying characteristics of the first generation of American single-seat jet fighters and the first US four-jet bomber.

Beamont's flight reports have always been models of their kind; explicit, analytical, straight to the point, sifting the essential from the merely interesting and bringing back to design teams practical views on what was required to advance nearer to perfection. Such skills were greatly appreciated in the United States, and Beamont's penetrating analyses of the good, and the not-so-good features of these aircraft make this book not only valuable, but also of absorbing interest, including, as they do, aircraft all the way from the pleasant Lockheed P-80 and the outstanding North American P-86, controllable up to Mach 1 (remarkable for 1948), to the lethal F-104 with its horrific downwards ejector seat.

With the Canberra successfully launched in 1949, Beamont was able to demonstrate its exceptional qualities when, in August 1952 he made the first one-day 'double-crossing' of the North Atlantic from Aldergrove to Gander and back — a distance of 3,636 nautical miles covered in an elapsed time of ten hours four minutes. Cruising at 47,000 feet at up to Mach 0.84, the two-way flying time was exactly eight hours, giving a block speed of 454 knots — way ahead of other aircraft of its time. As Beamont observed laconically, 'it had been an interesting day', including a telegram of congratulations from Her Majesty The Queen.

Such progress during the early post-War years served to throw into still greater perspective the ill-judged official decisions whereby, from 1947, the British aircraft industry and the Royal Air Force were forced to lag behind the United States in the development of aircraft capable of supersonic performance in level flight.

That situation was rectified on 11 August 1954, when, on his third flight of the new English Electric P.1 prototype, it became the first British aircraft to achieve Mach 1 in level flight — and with superb handling characteristics. The P.1B Lightning, a fighter capable of Mach 2.2 and 70,000 feet — steered forward by the team under Sir Frederick Page — went on to remain in front line service with the Royal Air Force for twenty-seven years, gained valuable export orders and came to be regarded as the finest all-weather fighter of its time: it was faster and more manoeuvrable than either the Mirage or the F-106 and had better handling qualities than any of its contemporaries. The Lightning and its team have never been as fully acclaimed as is their due.

Promise of translating these characteristics into the 'impossible specification' of the TSR-2 was shown to be within grasp when Beamont flew this twin-Olympus

BAC prototype (XR-219) at Boscombe Down on 27 September 1964. He took it to supersonic speeds on the fourteenth flight on 22 February 1965 at 30,000 feet, with no handling problems. As he reported, 'Flight conditions, supersonic, remained smooth and trim change free.' He adds, 'Twenty-five years later, the least that can be said is that the TSR-2 had demonstrated once again the formidable potential of Britain's aviation industry in the demanding field of aviation technology', and that 'but for the challenge and stimulus of the TSR-2, the technology vitally needed for the Tornado and the EFA might well have been unavailable in this country'.

Beamont concludes this splendid book with a laconic account of a run-of-the-mill flight from Heathrow to Washington, DC, on the flight deck of Concorde — flying at Mach 2 at 60,000 feet and at 530 knots IAS. 'There are very few military aircraft that could operate at this combination of speed and altitude — and none that could do so over mid-Atlantic without in-flight refuelling.'

This is a book to be savoured and re-read. It is written with insight and authority, while making light of the hazards inseparable from explorations on the frontiers of knowledge and is an outstanding record of services to British — and world — aviation. In its particular field it will be seen as one of the, still few, classics on aviation.

Peter Masefield

Introduction

The period immediately following World War II was one of major significance in aviation with the arrival of the practical gas turbine 'jet' engine and its potential for providing a vast increase in power-to-weight ratio and therefore efficiency.

Even while they were scaling down from mass wartime production, the aircraft manufacturers in Britain and America, soon to be followed by the rapidly rebuilding French industry, set out to develop fighter, and later bomber, designs based at first on the rather bulky centrifugal jet engines and then, as they became available, the axial-flow jets with their much reduced frontal area.

With only three exceptions these early jet developments performed disappointingly because, despite the increased power now readily available, their aerodynamic designs had not advanced sufficiently to make much impression on the 'compressibility barrier', with the result that they all encountered excessive drag, buffeting and control problems in the range Mach 0.7–0.8.

The exceptions included the DH.108 research aircraft, which achieved speeds in the dive under normal control up to M 0.98 and was eventually dived by John Derry in September 1948 at Mach 1+, though not under full control; and the North American XP86 fighter prototype which, by May 1948, was exploring Mach 1 in adequately controlled dives.

Before this the third exception had provided the historic breakthrough. In 1947 the Bell X-1 rocket-powered research aeroplane (air launched from a B-29 bomber), had reached and exceeded the speed of sound under conventional control in level flight in the hands of Captain Charles Yeager of the USAF. Sonic flight had been reached with safety, and now future military aviation would inevitably require supersonic capability and any nation without it would soon be out of the race.

In 1947 the UK Government, in the first of a series of inept political decisions which were to seriously constrain the growth and potential of British aviation technology over the next thirty years, cancelled the only existing programme for a British supersonic aircraft, the Miles M.2, and vetoed all further plans for the development of manned supersonic aircraft in Britain.

In the meantime the English Electric Company at Preston, with their airfields at Samlesbury and Warton, had been making good progress since 1945 in the development, to specification B3/45, of a very advanced, twin-jet military aircraft (which was to become the famous Canberra); such good progress in fact that, by 1947, there was confidence that the aircraft would fly by 1949 and, when it did, would be capable of operating at least 10,000 ft higher than contemporary fighters while at the same time being as fast as most of them.

It was becoming very clear that only a fighter with at least transonic performance would be capable of intercepting this new class of aeroplane. So, ignoring the current Government policy, the Warton design team, led by Teddy Petter, produced a series of design studies for a practical supersonic research aircraft with potential for development into an operational fighter, and by 1948 they were ready to present their results to the Ministries.

After much debate, including actual resistance from specialists at RAE Farnborough who were opposed to some aspects of English Electric's design philosophy, the Air Ministry issued contracts under specification F23/49 for two distinctly different designs: one to English Electric for its P.1, twin-engined, sixty-degree swept wing and low tailplane proposal, and the other to Fairey Aircraft Ltd for its single-engined, horizontal tailless Delta concept.

The competition for British military supersonic flight was on.

The events and experiences described in the following chapters show the main thrust of Britain's contribution to the evolution of supersonic flight which has at times been significant, but all too often has been prevented at critical periods from realising its full potential by the absence of consistent and resolute government support.

Indeed, one of Britain's greatest contributions to world aviation, the successful and unique supersonic Concorde airliner in partnership with France, came within an ace of cancellation by the 1964 Wilson Government who, when reminded of their contractual obligations by the French Government, then cancelled the TSR.2 instead!

Chapter One
First Experiences of Compressibility

The problems of the 'Sound Barrier' arose in the 1930s with the appearance of the first single-engined monoplane fighters with retractable undercarriages, namely the Hurricane, Spitfire and Me109.

The classic Spitfire shape. A 1942 period Mk. V seen here with a non-standard four blade propeller, landing at the Vickers test airfield at Wisley in 1964, in the hands of the author.

These aeroplanes, with maximum speeds exceeding 300 mph(T) and diving speeds around 400 mph(T), were a major advance on the biplanes which they replaced; but with their first stage engine developments their practical ceiling was about 30,000 ft and, in the early days at least, high speed diving tended to reach speed limits at well below 20,000 ft. Then, as experience was gained and increases in engine output became available, the performance boundaries were extended to higher altitudes and it was in this phase that some unexplained incidents began to be reported.

By 1943 diving into 'compressibility' had become a normal, though never mundane, event in the Typhoon testing programme at Hawker's Langley test centre. George Bulman, Chief Test Pilot, his deputy Philip Lucas and experimental test pilots Bill Humble, the author and, in particular, Ken Seth Smith, were engaged in a concentrated investigation into all normal and some very abnormal aspects of high

'Watty' Watson of 'A' Flight with a Hurricane I of No. 87 squadron at Exeter during the Battle of Britain in August 1940. This version has the Rotol constant speed propeller and eight .303 Browning machine guns. *(Watson Collection)*

speed diving aimed primarily at establishing the cause of a recent spate of fatal structural failures, apparently to the tail sections, which had in every case been found widely separated from the main wreckage.

One test flight at Langley on 16 October 1943 in Typhoon 1B, serial EK 152, was typical of the period and was described by the author:

> On 16 October 1943 I was detailed for the next flight in the Typhoon 'Strain-gauge' series of tests during which, in previous weeks I had reached a number of odd conditions, such as cutting the engine on the ignition switches from full power in a near-vertical dive at 500 mph IAS and then, with the tail still in place, repeating the exercise under negative 'g'. On this particular flight I was to begin to look at all these variations in the last unexplored corner of the flight envelope at the highest combination of indicated airspeed and altitude which could be reached. Flight test engineer Charlie Dunn briefed me that from a maximum power 'level' at 30,000 ft, a push-over into a near vertical dive should enable us to reach about 450 mph indicated at 20,000 ft. This, he said, would do for a start.
>
> It was a day of variable layered cloud as I sat in EK 152 behind the clattering, roaring Sabre engine with the 'saloon car' doors leaking vee-shaped draughts which utterly defeated the efforts of the cockpit hot air system to keep the pilot warm. At 28,000 ft there was no clear space in sight for the required dive but I levelled at 31,000 ft on top of a cirrus deck and pushed up the power to maximum boost and the phenomenal Sabre RPM limit of 3750 rpm. As speed built up a break occurred in the clouds to port and, at the bottom of a quite well defined cloud shaft, a bend in the Thames near Eton was visible. The hole looked just about big enough.
>
> Setting the instrumentation switches and noting the initial flight conditions on the test pad I rolled down to port, bringing the rpm back slightly as a margin against loss of propeller constant-speed control. Rolling out into a near-vertical

A production standard Typhoon 1b in the markings of the author as CO of No. 609 Squadron at Manston in 1943. The first stage improvement in rear vision can be seen, as can the lengthened cannon fairings — a local 'mod' by 609 Squadron! *(Ziegler Collection)*

dive, I trimmed the elevators with a slight residual push force as a safety margin and this time against the anticipated nose-down trim effects of compressibility. At 27,000 ft the general noise and fuss was becoming impressive with buffet vibration building up through the controls, seat and cockpit sides — even the 'motor car' windows were vibrating visibly at their natural frequency, and it was while observing this with interest that the situation developed suddenly. I was conscious of the controls stiffening up quite rapidly, of the port wing trying to drop and of the aircraft becoming nose-heavy to the accompaniment of violent buffeting and a general feeling of insecurity; and when beginning to bear back on the stick to hold the dive angle from getting too steep and holding off starboard aileron to maintain wings level, it was markedly apparent that these actions were becoming progressively less effective. A full two-handed pull failed to reduce the dive angle at all and we were now going downhill and rolling to port with maximum noise, buffet and general commotion, and with no conventional control of the situation at all. Here was this thing called 'compressibility' about which Philip Lucas had said, 'Whatever you do don't trim it out of the dive', as the consequent trim reversal during recovery would probably overstress something severely. So I didn't and throttling right back, continued to ride the shuddering and largely uncontrolled Typhoon down through 20,000 ft until passing about 15,000 ft. There, as the Mach number dropped at the still nearly constant indicated airspeed, the shock waves were supposed to subside allowing control effectiveness to recover. This indeed occurred, and with subsiding buffet aileron effectiveness recovered first enabling the wings to be levelled, then the nose began to rise under my still heavy pull-force until at last it was possible to ease off and recover to a level attitude, still with the throttle closed, the ASI dropping back from 500 mph and, impressively, the altimeter steadying at only 8500 ft.

This was the classic pattern of compressibility incident which was encountered subsequently, with minor variations according to type, on all the final generation of piston-engined fighters and the first generation of jets. But once again the tail

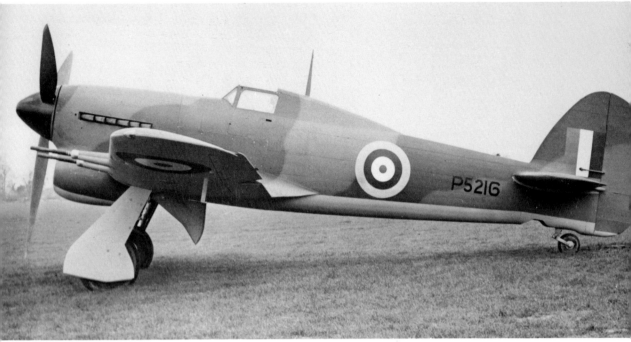

Two views of the second prototype Hawker Typhoon, which was first flown on 3 May 1941, modified with four 20-mm cannon. The pilot was Philip Lucas. This was the first Typhoon build to 'Mk. 1b' standard, and it still retained the total lack of rear vision. *(British Aerospace)*

had not come off, and even more imaginative flight conditions had to be tested before the Typhoon was finally cleared of any shadow of doubt that tail failures could have occurred as a result of normal or even extreme operating conditions.

In one of the ultimate tests, the schedule called for a maximum power dive to 500 mph indicated, trimmed out for propeller torque and high IAS effect and then, with the pilot's feet on the cockpit floor and away from the rudder pedals, the full throttle engine to be cut on the ignition switches. That this would produce a fin side-load approaching the design 'yaw' was anticipated, and the possibility that this might well be the condition that had brought the other tails off did not escape the pilot. It was, after all, a rather convenient solution as it fitted the background of engine unreliability which had plagued the Typhoon since its entry into squadron service in the previous year. But once again the tail did not fall off my aircraft as it had with Ken Smith's. Ultimately, the cause of the tail losses was traced positively to random fatigue failures of the elevator mass balance mountings, which had resulted in elevator flutter at high speed and the consequent structural failures.

During this period of intensive exploration of what was now being established as 'temporary but ultimately recoverable loss of control' (in most cases), George Bulman produced a memorandum: *'Compressibility: What it does and how to cope'* which was the first on the subject and of great value to all the establishments concerned at that time: RAE Farnborough; Supermarine; de Havilland; the Ministries; and, of course, the Hawker flight test team.

The Langley experience was paralleled at Farnborough where Aero Flight aerodynamicists Handel Davies, Morien Morgan and 'Dai' Morris (well known by the test pilots as the 'Welsh Mafia') were pioneering official British research into this phenomenon. In a programme conducted with skill and resolution, RAF test pilots of Aero Flight used the only suitable aircraft available — Spitfires. They were eventually to reach Mach numbers over 0.9 in violent out-of-control dives which, on two occasions, resulted in the catastrophic failure of the reduction gears and loss (off the aircraft!) of propellers — the Spitfires being skilfully force-landed, regardless.

Compressibility in Germany

German experience was similar and had begun even before the war. On 17 July 1937 Messerschmitt's test pilot, Dr Kurt Jodlbauer, was scheduled to demonstrate a 'terminal dive' in a Bayerische Flugzeugwerke Messerschmitt 109 with a Jumo 210 engine, at the Rechlin test centre. Jodlbauer had been advised to approach the test point in steps and not to re-trim in the dive. The 109 entered a vertical dive at 5000 metres from which it never recovered and it crashed into Lake Müritz, killing the pilot.

This was almost certainly the first accident caused by 'compressibility', the phenomenon of airflow break-down into shock waves as the speed of sound is approached, which needed more than a decade of research and design evolution and took the lives of many fighter pilots and test pilots before the problems of what later became widely known as the 'Sound Barrier' were finally resolved.

Following this incident speed limits were imposed on the 109, and when the 109E,

Messerschmitt Me 109B with 680 PS Jumo Vilmo 210 engine. An early development version similar to the aircraft which first encountered 'compressibility' in 1937.
(Deutsches Museum, Munich)

incorporating a DB601 engine, was introduced into Luftwaffe service in 1939 it was limited to 750 Kmph at sea level and correspondingly less at altitude. But as soon as operations began against the RAF over England in 1940/41, the *Luftwaffe* reported incidents of loss of control in diving when the set limits were often greatly exceeded in battle; and many seemingly unexplained accidents were thought to have resulted.

The *Reichsluftfahrtministerium* (German Air Ministry) ordered Rechlin to investigate on high priority, and official test pilots undertook this hazardous work. Writing in 1981 Heinrich Beauvais, senior fighter development test pilot at Rechlin during the war years, remembered:

> I intended, on the first test to dive vertically from 9000 metres altitude to a speed of 750 Kmph on the ASI (I could expect to reach this speed at 6000 metres, thus allowing a good magin above normal practice). I went into the dive by half-rolling and tried to pull out at 750 Kmph, but a small frozen lake — it was January 1941 — refused to disappear from my field of view. So, a case of Jodlbauer, thought I. Despite some misgivings regarding the strength of the controls, I decided to pull with all my strength and failing that, to try to pull out by trimming (tailplane). The application of force sufficed; the 109 was returned to horizontal by about 4000 metres.
>
> The flight, as a preliminary test, was not measured from the ground, and no

recorders or cameras had been installed in the aircraft. I cannot say by how much the indicated speed of 750 Kmph was exceeded.

After this result, I was at first forbidden to carry out any further similar tests. It was first required to obtain some clearer understanding of the phenomena, e.g. by comparison with the investigation into Jodlbauer's accident and with wind tunnel tests etc. It was also intended that further tests be conducted with safety devices such as dive brakes, ejection seat etc. *(The first successful ejection seat escape system was developed for the FW 190, and became operational in 1942.)*

My flight was actually contrary to the basic (Rechlin) principle for high-risk flights, which was that the E-Stelle *(Official Flight Trials Unit)* would only perform such flights after clearance by the industry*. Jodlbauer's flight had taken place in the service of the Bayerische Flugzeugwerke Messerschmitt.

I had the impression of very high stick forces, which I only applied after due consideration. I believe that I can now remember, however, that some pilots had stated that in the compressibility dive the stick could be moved without force. I regarded that as improbable or rather as nonsense, for later on, in diving the 190 at over 850 Kmph (at low altitude) and the Me 262 at around 1000 Kmph, there was always an onset of high stick forces. Nobody spoke any more about zero-force control movement.

The first operational version of the FW 190A-3. This aircraft of 11/JG26 was landed in error at RAF Pembrey in Spring 1943 by Oberleutnant Armin Faber, and subsequently evaluated at Farnborough by Service test pilots, including the author. *(IWM)*

---

* Similar to the rules for C.A. RELEASE testing at Boscombe Down, then and today.

After Jodlbauer's accident, much attention was given to questions concerning elevators and horizontal tail surfaces generally. Elastic deformation was studied (Dr Fingado) and it was found that with high elevator loads (400 kg?), the tail surface could no longer be trimmed. In my case it did not come to the point of trimming, but I cannot report on the loads. After my test of 1941, the first one to talk of Mach effects was, to the best of my knowledge, Multhopp (then with Focke-Wulf, and after the war in the USA). In my case, the question which was often discussed and never clearly answered was whether the decisive factor in pulling out (of the dive) was the stick force (or elevator deflection) or the increasing air density. So far as I know, on no aircraft type were systematic terminal dive tests carried out at that time, although they were wanted. Experience at high speeds was, however, accumulated in the course of years. I heard no more of accidents in dives after that. There were nevertheless indications of the need for caution. For example, from wind tunnel tests it appeared that after the nose-heavy change of trim, further increase of speed could be expected to produce a strong nose-up trim change (Kuchemann after the war at RAE?). This would have been a kind of instability which (from experiences with instability as a result of aft CG and at speeds around 650 Kmph) would have been catastrophic. (I do not know to this day whether this conclusion from wind tunnel tests was proved to be correct — perhaps for the normal aerofoil profiles of that time? Present-day supersonic aircraft of course do not show this characteristic). *Author's note: In 1950 the Canberra demonstrated this nose-up pitch at Mach 0.86 when held through the Mach 0.84 nose-down change.*

One day when I was in Berlin, a colleague — Neidhart — was killed for no explained reason in a 190 in which I had, the day before, carried out dives up to almost 900 Kmph. I have wondered again and again whether those dives brought about changes to the aircraft which would have led to the accident. In that case though, why did nothing happen to me, or why did I notice nothing?

The first prototype Focke Wulf 190 V1 with BMW-139 engine, with the ducted spinner which was later abandoned in favour of a conventional radial cowling with additional fan-cooling. *(Deutsches Museum, Munich)*

With the Me 262, the onset of nose-heaviness did not occur until 1000 Kmph or more. It was sometimes observed but as far as I know was not systematically investigated, although the intention to do so was there. The higher speed, compared with the 109, was probably an effect of the wing sweep of the 262. With this type one had worries about the strength of the canopy at high speed. Jettison tests with a fuselage were carried out, as were towed tests in water. At that time, I put the question to the aerodynamicists as to whether the onset of Mach effects could be forecast by taking pressure measurements on certain parts of the wing.

The loss of effectiveness of high tailplanes/elevators in the 'deep stall' is quite another matter. For this reason were the tailplanes of Lightning and Tornado set low!

Experience in England had been very similar. During the Battle of Britain Spitfire and Hurricane pilots had often reported temporary loss of elevator control when diving at high speed in combat, and there were cases of unexplained crashes with no evidence of battle damage.

The four 20-mm Hispano cannon development on a Hurricane IIc of No. 87 squadron in night-black finish, flown by the CO, Squadron Leader 'Splinters' Smallwood, from Charmey Down in 1941. *(IWM)*

In 1942 George Bulman of Hawker Aircraft stressed the vital need to maintain a steady and strong pull force on the elevator during the 'uncontrolled' phase of the 'compressibility' dive 'until recovery occurs at lower altitude', and on no account to 'trim out of the dive'.

By the end of 1942, relevant and repeatable experience was being obtained with the new Sabre-engined Typhoon fighter which could now easily achieve 'compressibility' by 24,000 ft in a vertical dive from 30,000 ft. At about 450 mph IAS all longitudinal response was lost accompanied by very heavy buffeting until, generally below 15,000 ft, the nose would begin to rise and level flight was regained at around 12,000 ft. This all happened at about Mach 0.74 and was seen as a positive limit to practical fighter operations, but in Germany progress was more rapid. The emergent swept-wing jet and rocket fighters, the Me 262 and 163, were already achieving Mach 0.8+ in their test programmes but they were again encountering symptoms of buffet, pitch-trim change and loss of elevator effectiveness similar to the now established characteristics of the 109 at slower speeds.

Mano Zeigler, senior test pilot of the Me 262 programme recalled:

> The testing took place where only chance or luck decided between life or death. The pilots climbed to 10,000–12,000 metres altitude and went into a steep dive at full throttle, reaching a speed of about 950 Kmph at about 7000 metres height. This was, at that height, near to the speed of sound. This announced itself by the aircraft nosing over into an even steeper flight path, and by a deep rumbling noise

The Messerschmitt 262, the first successful jet fighter, whose compressibility characteristics were described by test pilot Mano Zeigler. *(Flight International)*

in the cockpit which, increasing more and more, finally sounded like a long-lasting roll of thunder. Shortly before the onset of this thundering noise, the speed of the Me 262 increased even higher until, without any further warning, the aircraft, with a sudden lurch, tipped over to one side. Then came a dangerous situation for machine and pilot alike, for the Me now plunged down out of control. The pilot did not know when the separated flow would re-attach to the wings and control surfaces and when the aircraft would again obey the latter. It happened sooner or later, but often at such a low altitude that the test pilot would have barely two to three hundred metres below him on regaining horizontal flight.

It was a game for nerves of steel, which was played here for the first time.

The thin swept wing of the 262 enabled it to reach its critical compressibility threshold at Mach 0.83 in a shallow dive from 8000 metres with a height loss of 2000 metres. The nose then dropped requiring a pull force of 15 kg to hold it. With speed still increasing as the nose dropped further. Mach 0.86 was reached at about 5700 metres (approx. 1000 Kmph) and a pull force of about 45 kg was needed to prevent a further increase in dive angle and speed. No effective cure could be found and in *Luftwaffe* service the 262 was limited to a 'never-exceed' IAS of 950 Kmph.

The Gloster Meteor I, the RAF's first jet fighter, seen here at Manston, with No. 616 Squadron in summer 1944. *(IWM)*

Preparing to fly a 616 Squadron Meteor I at Manston in 1944. *(IWM)*

A Meteor I in landing configuration at Manston. *(IWM)*

When the 262 began reaching operational units in early 1944 not only was it the first operational jet fighter in the world, but it also had a significantly higher critical Mach number than the British Gloster Meteor which followed it into squadron service in August of that year. (No. 616 Squadron, based at Manston.)

In the same period, the Me 163 rocket fighter also became operational with a never-exceed speed of 900 Kmph to keep it clear of a severe pitching oscillation in compressibility at around Mach 0.8.

In 1943 the first British jet fighters, the Meteor I and III in the hands of Michael Daunt of Glosters and Group Captain 'Willy' Wilson of RAE Farnborough, encountered very similar 'compressibility' problems, but at the significantly lower critical Mach numbers of between 0.71 and 0.74, due to flow breakaway at the wing root coupled with high drag from the barrel-shaped nacelles of the relatively bulky Rolls-Royce Welland and Derwent centrifugal-flow jet engines. This was disappointing and after extensive wind-tunnel testing, longer improved fineness-ratio engine nacelles enabled the Meteor IV to reach Mach Crit. 0.84 and a service clearance of Mach 0.8 — but not before the war had ended.

By 1945 at the commencement of the post-war surge in jet fighter development by the Allies, Germany which was by then out of the running had already established a significant lead over the rest of the world with a successful and formidable jet fighter whose limiting Mach number would not be matched by any other aircraft in RAF squadron service until the introduction of the Canberra (service limit Mach 0.84; Mach Crit 0.86) in 1950.

Meteor Shock Stall

In early 1946 while briefly based at Moreton Valence as senior project pilot for Glosters on the Meteor IV development programme, the author was responsible for the clearance testing of a Meteor IV specially prepared for an attempt on the World Air Speed Record by the RAF's High Speed Flight; and this produced some further interesting experience of 'Compressibility.'

At Moreton Valence in Spring 1946 the much improved fineness-ration nacelles (compared with those of Meteor III) on the Derwent V-engined Meteor IV had resulted in a further small increase in usable Mach number; and in an intensive series of dives to the out-of-control condition in March-April, mainly in *EE 455*, the author found that Mach 0.79 was the new boundary of reasonable control.

By Mach 0.83–0.84 there was powerful pitch-down with no response to elevator and the consequent dive had to be ridden down in violent buffeting until passing about 15,000 ft, where the nose began to rise slowly under continued heavy pull-force as the Mach number reduced with loss of altitude. This was a finite limitation which no Meteor IV was going to exceed operationally for any practical purpose — but it was restricting only in diving as the level thrust/drag performance maximum of about Mach 0.78 at the tropopause could be reached without serious control trouble, although buffet and the beginnings of compressibility trim changes were in evidence. But the margins were small and squadron pilots would now have to be trained in the technique for descents keeping clear of 'compressibility.'

The two special Meteor IVs prepared for the 1945 World Air Speed Record attempt. Eric Greenwood is in EE 454. *(British Aerospace)*

At about this time a special Meteor Meteor IV with clipped wingtips was being prepared, with a spare aircraft, for testing to at least 10 mph in excess of the existing record (set the previous year by Group Captain 'Willy' Wilson in Meteor IV *EE 454*), plus as great a safety margin as proved practical.

It fell to the author to conduct these trials at Moreton Valence in July, but first a Meteor IV, *EE 455*, was taken to Boscombe Down for airspeed indicator calibration tests. These were carried out on 12 June, 1946, with a Farnborough-supplied barograph installed, and the Meteor was flown past kine-theodolites mounted on highpoints on hangars and the headquarters building at about 60 ft above ground. This provided some quite exhilarating flying as the progressive high speed runs, starting at 557 mph IAS (Indicated Air Speed), reached the maximum found practical in these conditions at 580 mph. When corrected, a massive 'position-error' of +17 mph was established; this meant that the fastest run had been only 9 mph short of the existing record. To obtain the true speed of 616+ mph required for a new record, an IAS of about 600 mph would need to be achieved as an average of one run in each direction on the day.

Back at Moreton Valance, *EE 549* was fitted with uprated Derwent V engines and tested in stages to 595 mph IAS at 1000 ft, and then progressively lower reaching 605 mph IAS at 700 ft. At these speeds the noise level was impressive and the controls were noticeably stiffening, but response on all three axes was adequate and the decision was taken, firstly to set up 605 mph at 500 ft and then, if practicable, take it down in a shallow descent at full power to reach an absolute thrust/drag maximum at 100 ft above the Severn estuary in the over-water conditions specified for the RAF attempt which was eventually to be made off Littlehampton.

All these tests were ambient temperature-sensitive, being at the thrust/drag boundary, and to achieve the highest IAS at the lowest Mach drag a hot day was needed. On 9 July, with a Met temperature of +27°C, *EE 549* was initially dived down the Severn over the Aust Ferry to 595 mph IAS at 200 ft to assess turbulence. Conditions were dead calm with good visibility in bright sunshine and so, with a final tightening of harness straps and a health-check of engine instruments, the Meteor was pulled up in a starboard turn over the Welsh bank of the Severn and rolled back southwest to line up over Aust and down the centre of the river towards Avonmouth with throttles wide open.

At 500 ft and IAS at 600 mph and increasing, a final elevator trim adjustment was made and then the stick was eased back, passing 200 ft at 608 mph IAS, as the water began to look very close. Then it happened. With a noticeable tuck-down the nose dropped, and an adrenalin-inspired, two-handed pull on the stick did not achieve the urgently needed response. With no chance to look again at the airspeed which was still increasing, the water was now a flashing blur immediately below, and this was 'crisis corner'. In the seconds before what looked like imminent impact it was quite clear what was happening — this was 'compressibility' at sea level!

Knowledge that throttling back would only increase the nose-down moment, left nothing else but to pull hard with both hands and hope. Gradually, the nose began to rise and the Meteor flew clear. It had been a close thing indeed and on the way back to Moreton Valence, sweating from the heat of the high-speed run and the physical effort of the pull-out, and with a heightened adrenalin level, two things became clear: Compressibility could be reached in this Meteor IV in only a shallow descent at low altitude, and this would have to be guarded against in future; furthermore, whatever true speed came out of the correction of this test point, there was no way that this aircraft would fly faster than that!

In the event, the flight-test engineers found that the corrected maximum true speed was 632 mph, and when Gloster's publicity department heard of this they immediately leaked it to the Press with results which were unfortunate and embarrassing, because it had not been an official record and also because there was no way in which the RAF could set as high a figure in their forthcoming trial, as this would have to be carried out within safety limits recommended and approved by the Company.

EE 549 was delivered to Tangmere in early August with a formal Vne (never exceed speed) of 600 mph IAS which, corrected, would give 614–618 mph TAS (True Air Speed), depending on the temperature of the day. When Gp Capt Teddy Donaldson skilfully broke the record again for Britain off Littlehampton in September, it was at 616 mph TAS.

The record attempt clearance trials had the valuable effect of contributing further to the knowledge of the flight envelope boundary of the Meteor IV, and it was now possible to plot the absolute limits of control in indicated Mach number at close height intervals from sea level to about 35,000 ft. Above this the g-stall/shock-stall boundaries closed sharply towards each other with the increase in altitude, but although it was soon realised that this would impose much more severe limitations on practical interception operations than implied by the manufacturer's quoted 'operational ceiling — 45,000 ft', the actual boundaries had not been plotted.

From 1947-48, English Electric carried out trials at Warton, using a Meteor IV (serial EE 545) under special contract to explore and establish these limits in the remaining corner of the flight envelope from 35,000 to 45,000 ft; and, together with the previous Moreton Valence tests, evidence was obtained by the end of 1947 from more than 60 dives in Meteor IVs into the shock-stall, many of which resulted in delayed recovery to below 15,000 ft before being able to regain level flight. These trials were carried out to, or in some instances beyond, the conventional limits of safety, and at that time the Meteor IV was probably the first type to have its absolute limits of compressibility plotted so comprehensively from sea level to operational ceiling; but it was a programme typical of the probing more or less into the unknown which characterised compressibility investigation and testing in those years.

Scientists thought they knew what was happening to airflow around airframes at eighty per cent of the speed of sound and what would happen at 100 per cent, but test pilots were not quite so convinced as they continued to fall out of the sky in unsuitable aeroplanes with the maximum of buffeting commotion, violent trim changes, and unresponsive controls. As a rhyme, written by test pilot Michael Daunt and circulated from Gloster's pilots' office to the design office at Bentham, put it:

> Sing a song of shock-stall, words by Ernest Mach
> Four-and-twenty slide-rules shuffling in the dark.

Between 1945 and 1949 the fighter industry world-wide was preoccupied with

A DH Vampire I demonstrated by the author at the SBAC/RAeS display at Radlett on 13 September 1946. *(British Aerospace)*

The developed P1081 with fully swept tail. Wade was killed in this aircraft in 1949. *(Flight International)*

The DH 108 experimental aircraft in 1947. It was in the second prototype, TG 306, that Geoffrey de Havilland was killed in September 1946. *(Flight International)*

The second prototype Hawker Tempest V at the Langley factory in late 1943 immediately prior to despatch to Boscombe Down for Service Trials. This aircraft has the 'long' cannon protruding from the wing leading edge. *(British Aerospace)*

A production Tempest V series 2, with 'short' cannon and provision for long-range 'drop-tanks', being flown by Bill Humble from Langley in 1944. *(British Aerospace)*

An improved Tempest VI at Langley in 1945 with 'short' cannon and hard-points for underwing drop-tanks or bombs, and uprated engine. *(British Aerospace)*

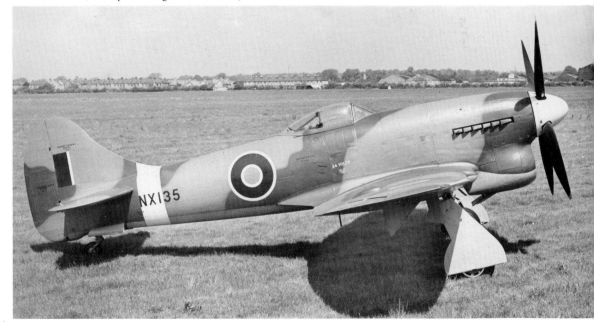

A fine air-shot of a Langley factory-fresh Tempest V with Bill Humble, in 1944. *(British Aerospace)*

'getting through the barrier', but the majority of companies failed to achieve success.

Hawker, de Havilland, Vickers and Gloster (UK); Breguet and Dassault (France); Northrop, Republic and Chance Vought (USA); and SAAB (Sweden); all these companies had followed the German experience and developed and flew jet fighter prototypes with varying degrees of wing leading-edge sweep-back to delay the effects of compressibility; and with a wide variety of tail configurations from medium/low tailplanes to the high 'Tee' tail which proved to be no solution at all and resulted in the loss of some aircraft in 'deep stall' tests.

With exceptions, like the SAAB J29 and the Republic P-84 series, all these developments had wing-root or fuselage-side air-intakes which, together with the relatively thick wings of the period, resulted in excessive profile drag and compressibility limitations in the range Mach 0.74 to 0.8. This was disappointing and involved much uncomfortable and hazardous test flying as company test pilots Neville Duke, 'Wimpey' Wade and Frank Murphy of Hawker; Geoffrey de Havilland and John Derry of de Havilland; Mike Lithgow of Supermarine; and John Crosby Warren, Michael Daunt, and later the author, at Gloster, pressed on diving to the limits of control, and often beyond into complete loss of control at high altitude before recovering in the denser air at lower level. Geoffrey de Havilland and 'Wimpey' Wade were killed in these trials.

These experiences were not unique and were repeated in all the world-wide fighter developments of the period, with the notable exception of the North American P-86 Sabre which, in 1948, became the first fighter to demonstrate the ability to dive to the speed of sound under controlled conditions.

Therefore the first generation of jets entered service in the immediate post-War years with little increase in dive performance over their propeller-driven predecessors; for example the Mach 0.74 limit of the post-War Vampire actually compared unfavourably with the Mach 0.76 capability of the Tempest V some years earlier! Nevertheless, despite the set-backs the new technology of the jets provided interesting test flying in what was still a subsonic period, and reports on some of those flown by the author are reproduced on the following pages.

Chapter Two
Testing First Generation American Jets

Following the Meteor experiences, and in the period of preparation for the forthcoming test programmes on English Electric's B3/45 jet bomber prototype, the author carried out a series of handling evaluations on some of the newly emerging American military jets, arranged by the Ministry of Aircraft Production.

The first aircraft flown was the Lockheed P-80 'Shooting Star' at the USAF's Wright-Patterson Test Centre, following a briefing by Dick Johnson and Bob Hoover. (Both were to become famous test pilots over the next two decades. Hoover becoming arguably the world's most accomplished display pilot.)

Flight Report on Lockheed P-80 No. AF460 (IXI 40) at Patterson Field USAF Base, 14 May 1948.

This aircraft, which has a wing loading of forty-nine pounds per square foot at take-off, behaves in a manner reminiscent of the Meteor IV in that there is little tendency to 'snake' until quite high indicted speeds are reached; ailerons are very light and powerful (with servodyne) while elevators and rudder become very heavy with speed. Manoeuvrability is therefore a combination of extremes from the operational aspect in that the turning circle is relatively poor at all speeds and heights, while the rates of roll are as high as with any other production aircraft in the world.

At 450 mph IAS, 5000 ft, I noted 3–4 sec/360° as the best of three maximum rate rolls attempted during this flight, and was afterwards assured that I was not achieving full control angles. During this flight I was not able to time the climb to 30,000 ft accurately, owing to inclement weather, but the rate of climb did not appear in any way outstanding.

At Mach 0.8 a certain amount of vibration was evident at 30,000 ft and, at this height and Mach number, 2g seemed to be the most that could be held without the onset of the compressibility stall. A second flight will be necessary to confirm this, but my impression is that the 2g curve would peak at about 32,000 ft.

Level flight in rough air at 1000 ft produced 530 mph IAS, while a dive to 570 mph IAS produced no unusual characteristics except slight snaking. This aircraft and all the others at Patterson are fitted with a length of cord, fixed at one end on the top of the nose, which streams in flight along a line painted in front of the windscreen giving, theoretically, an indication of the onset of snaking.

The elevator, aileron and rudder trim tabs are operated electrically by separate switches, the elevator by a serrated push switch on the stick. This is well placed and the switch action would be satisfactory if the mecanism responded suitably. However, there is an unfortunate delay in response, followed by a too-rapid trim change so that trim has to be applied in a series of very small jerks if violent over-corrections are to be avoided. This is a very important point from the pilot's aspect in this type of control.

The rudder and aileron trim three-position switches function satisfactorily. The seat and stick relative positions are very poor indeed — my right arm, back and ankles were aching badly after half an hour; all pilots complain of this.

The grouping of cockpit instruments is very sketchy, and while all essential controls can be reached or read, there appears to have been little or no attempt at 'sense grouping'. One item of equipment worth special mention is the radio compass. This instrument cannot be praised too highly for the assistance which it can give to the short-endurance, high-speed aircraft pilot under IFR and even VFR conditions. The dive brakes were poor by British standards, being relatively ineffective in operation.

On landing at 128 mph (recommended speed 125 mph) the nosewheel tyre burst, but, after some curious manoeuvres, the aircraft was persuaded to maintain a straight course down the runway and no further damage resulted.

Conclusions

The Shooting Star has only one feature outstanding among modern fighter aircraft, and that is they very high rate of roll provided by the servodyne-assisted ailerons. This is of the order of 120°/sec at 450 mph IAS and sets a standard difficult to improve upon.

Apart from that, its general characteristics can be summarised best by saying that its performance is comparable to that of the Vampire III, its manoeuvrability to that of the Meteor IV, and its altitude characteristics inferior to both.

The layout of cockpit, seat and controls is the worst I have experienced for a long time, and the forward vision is poor in comparison with British practice during the past five or six years.

It is possible that the P-80 may be given a new lease of life with a more powerful engine, but such a move could not give it operational value above 35,000–38,000 ft unless steps are taken to reduce the wing loading and increase the limiting Mach number.

The nosewheel tyre-burst incident resulted in some hesitation on the following day in the Flight Test Centre, on the basis that 'maybe this Limey pilot is not competent'; and perhaps I did not react too wisely by expressing regret in the normal 'British' way for bursting the tyre, which was probably going to burst anyway! Colonel Al Boyd responded with the classic 'Don't apologise; it's a sign of weakness!'

There followed a short hiatus while Dick Johnson apparently persuaded Boyd that I should be allowed to continue with the planned programme; then, by the afternoon, the Colonel's authority was given for two P-84 Thunderjet flights, and I carried these out from Wright Field.

The next day the Republic Thunderjet was found to be an excellent fighter with a performance generally similar to the Meteor IV, but with a slightly higher maximum speed, superior combat manoeuvrability and, unlike the Meteor, superb all-round visibility.

The Americans by this time had applied the valuable experience gained in World War II to the designs of all their XP- series of post-war jet fighters which, without exception, were fitted with high quality, one-piece plexiglass canopies, in marked contrast to the heavy iron-ware of the mixed construction cockpit transparencies of the first British jet fighters.

Flight Reports on P-84s Nos. 514 and 515, Wright Field, 15 and 17 May 1948
I was pleasantly surprised with this aircraft which has a wing loading of fifty-one pounds per square foot and a reputation in some quarters of being 'more difficult than the P-80', but which is being introduced as a standard fighter aircraft into the USAF.

Unsticking at about 135 mph IAS without flaps in about 1000 yds, it soon proved to be a very pleasant aircraft in every way; in climb, inferior to the Meteor IV, in general manoeuvrability far superior, though inferior to the Vampire in this respect, except in rate of roll.

Two minutes of level flight at 1000 ft at 100 per cent power produced 568 mph IAS in rough air.

Ailerons were agreeably light at this speed, though the rudder and elevator were heavy. A shallow dive to 595 mph IAS (diving limitation 608 mph) gave the impression that the machine was perfectly happy at this speed — as indeed I was with it.

At 10,000 ft at 542 mph IAS, flight was perfectly smooth with no indication of compressibility vibration.

Use was not made of aileron boost as I could not locate the selection switch on this flight, but at 450 mph IAS 3–4 sec for 360 degrees was again regarded as a low roll rate by the test pilots of the fighter Test Division, Wright Field.

Under the existing conditions I could not detect any tendency towards snaking and gained an impression that it may well be a good gun platform.

Control characteristics near the stall are excellent and although the 'g-break' (accelerated stall) occurs at 1.5g/130–135 mph, the circuit and final approach are completely viceless at 140 mph.

Elevator control power at low speeds is such that the tail can be touched during the landing run and this has to be watched otherwise the landing is pleasantly simple.

Like the P-80, the -84 tends to roll for some distance once the nosewheel is on the ground; and though the foot-pedal brakes are quite effective, I would say that 2,500 yds would be the safe minimum for training purposes for this aircraft.

During this flight there was insufficient time to climb above 30,000 ft, but at this height it was not possible to sustain 2g at Mach 0.8. Maximum Mach number reached was 0.82 at which there was a tendency to nose-up trim change.

One feature common to both 140 and TG 180 engines is their poor acceleration and deceleration.

These characteristics are sufficiently pronounced to make an unexpected overshoot difficult, and to necessitate extra care in approach judgement.

17 May: P-84 No. 514
Timed climb at maximum continuous climb power:

Take-off	Zero min	IAS
10,000 ft	3⅓	312 mph
20,000 ft	6⅔	280 mph
30,000 ft	12⅔	260 mph
35,000 ft	18	240 mph
38,000 ft	22½	190 mph

These times are probably on the high side owing to the lack of experience on this type, but the rate of climb with exisiting thrust is definitely poor, while the aircraft is very sensitive to speed and climb angle (no climb at all was registered at 200 mph/35,000 ft/100 per cent power).

The highest Mach number reached was approximately 0.83, and a nose-up change of trim was noted at .825 without buffet.

Generally, the aircraft responded more effectively to the controls above 35,000 ft than the Meteor IV, but the high wing loading has the effect of reducing the peak of 2g manoeuvrability to the relatively low altitude of about 30,000 ft.

With the existing power unit the ceiling is reputed to be in the neighbourhood of 45,000 ft, but I would say that that figure is the absolute limit of flight and bears little relation to the maximum operational height.

Stalls were carried out at 10,000 ft and were found to occur straight, with a tendency to drop gently to starboard at 123 mph, gear up, and 116 mph, gear down (power off).

Cockpit vision

The available angle of vision over the nose is excellent, but forward vision is spoilt by heavily constructed windscreen and quarter panel frames. With the gyro gunsight in position, eighty per cent of vision through the front panel is degraded, and the final approach and landing has to be made through curved quarter panels, at a shallower angle to the line of sight than would be accepted in the UK; and which, because of distortion, provided quite inadequate forward vision for an aircraft of this landing performance when the gyro gunsight is fitted.

Conclusion

The Thunderjet is a viceless aircraft with a high performance potential and should achieve much popularity.

It is underpowered at the moment, but should become a first-class fighter weapon with the introduction of the TG 190.

This engine should provide it with an initial rate of climb in excess of 7000 ft/ min and a speed of over 600 mph, but the aircraft's high wing loading is likely to prevent its effective operational use above 35,000–38,000 ft.

With the more powerful engine endurance and range will compare approximately with current American practice.

High hopes are held in USAF circles for the sweep-back version of this aircraft, which is believed to be under construction (F-84F).

The next fixture in this interesting American programme was a 2000-mile flight across the States from Dayton, Ohio, to Muroc Air Force Base in the Mojave Desert, California. This took place on 18 May 1948 in a World War II-vintage North American B-25 light bomber, and at 6.45 pm when joining the circuit over the wide expanse of the flat salt-lake, golden in the evening sunshine, I could see a strange silver shape between hangars on the north side of the base. It had swept-back wings and tail surfaces — the XP-86, which I was going to fly!

But first I had a full day of briefing on the North American XB-45 Tornado — an advanced, four-engined, jet bomber which was under early developmental testing, and which seemed to be the nearest US equivalent to our own light jet bomber concept, the English Electric B3/45.

On 20 May I took part in a scheduled test flight of the third prototype, with the senior project test pilot, George Krebs, and made the following report: *(Overleaf.)*

Flight report on North American XB-45 No. 1001 at North American Flight Test Section, Muroc Lake, 20 May 1984

Power Plant: 4, TG 180 (sea level thrust 4,000 lb)

Gross weight (LR case):	85,700 lb
Fuel (LR case):	4600 US gal (3400 internal, 1200 in bomb bay drop tank)
Bomb Load (LR case):	10,000 lb
Crew:	Three

Range

Radius of action with ten per cent reserve (maker's estimate not corroborated by service trials): 842 miles. This figure is based on the following:

1. Weight as above
2. Take-off, climb 27,000 ft climb power
3. Cruise to 31,000 ft
4. Target 31,000 ft
5. Six minutes' 'evasion' to 34,500 ft
6. Cruise to 38,000 ft (cruise-climb)
7. Descent at 1800 ft/min
8. Average consumption 930 gal/hr
9. True speed 390 mph
10. Still-air distance 1660 miles
11. Time 4.28 hr
12. Fuel used 3950 US gal

Radius with 22,000 lb: 500 miles

Proven performance

Max speed:	536 mph 16,000 ft
Max range (LR case):	2230 miles at 350 mph
Twin-engined ceiling:	15,000 ft (most probably light)
Take-off over 50 ft:	5378 ft at 143 mph
Landing over 50 ft:	2880 ft

Strength Factors

Ultimate:	FourG
Design load:	ThreeG
Flight:	2.67g at design speed above 7000 ft
Flight:	2.5g at Mach 0.8
Flight:	−1.5g at design speed above 7000 ft

The flight consisted of a scheduled series of tests on low-speed and accelerated stability and tank-venting dives. I was permitted to fly the aircraft throughout, except during the specific tests.

Start-up

This was a lengthy process and took fifteen minutes before the aircraft was ready to taxi.

Taxying

The steerable nosewheel helped this operation considerably, although the actuator is slow at present and is to be geared up. Steering is by normal-sense steering-wheel action with the wheel positioned on the forward side of the left console.

Two views of the North American XB45 Tornado, on test from the USAF test centre at Muroc dry lake, California, in 1948. *(North American)*

Take-off (all-up weight approx 69,000 lb)
From the co-pilot's seat this operation might have been a little complicated but was in fact very simple and straightforward.

The aircraft was held straight by nosewheel steering up to eighty miles per hour, at which point the rudder becomes effective. The nosewheel was eased off at 110 mph and the unstick occurred at about 140 mph without any further effort.

The ailerons were noted to be particularly effective at, and immediately after, take-off, for a relatively large aicraft. Two take-offs were made from the co-pilot's seat, where direct forward vision is obscured by the pilot's ejection seat, and these were surprisingly simple.

The aircraft was then trimmed at climbing power (ninety-six per cent) and climbed to 10,000 ft where stalls were carred out clean and gear down. These were straight in both instances and occurred at the following speeds:

Undercarriage and flaps down:
110 mph and little warning, Aileron control still available.

Undercarriage and flaps up:
125 mph. Warning by elevator buffet from 132 mph and becoming violent near stall.

During this test, considerable aileron boost chatter was experienced at large aileron angles. This trouble had apparently been evading solution for some time.

Some rudder vibration had been experienced and on this flight a beaded strip had been applied to the top trailing edge of the rudder.

The aircraft was dived to the following conditions, and the vibrations could not be felt:

IAS	HEIGHT
400 mph	10,000 ft
450 mph	8100 ft
465 mph	7300 ft
480 mph	6500 ft
500 mph	6000 ft
500 mph	5000 ft (rough air)

I took over again at this point and climbed at the following recommended conditions (all max cruise ninety-six per cent):

IAS	HEIGHT	CLIMB RATE
260 mph	15,000 ft	1800 ft/min
250 mph	20,000 ft	1650 ft/min
240 mph	22,000 ft	1500 ft/min
240 mph	25,000 ft	1000 ft/min

At 26,000 ft at ninety-six per cent power, 240 mph, the JPTs were approximately 600, 610, 540 and 620 degrees; climb was continued at ninety-eight per cent until, at 30,000 ft, 190 mph IAS, the rate of climb was again down to 1000 ft/min. At this height and condition the aircraft was reasonably stable and responsive, but I gained the impression that an operational load would make a very great deal of difference to its handling there.

The next scheduled tests consisted of accelerated stability, and pull-outs were made up to 2g at 330 mph/25,000 ft. Compressibility buffeting was noted coming in at Mach 0.77.

From this point I took over again and climbed the aircraft back to 30,000 ft, preparatory to carrying out a dive to 15,000 ft at high Mach number for tank venting, which I was to do myself.

With power off, the dive had to be steep to reach Mach 0.77, and this was attained at about 23,000 ft and held until the pull-out at 15,000 ft. buffeting at this speed was not strong, but enough to leave the impression that there was not very far to go.

The pull-out was a simple matter with the powerful spring tab elevator and there is little doubt, as North American Aviation freely admit, that the pilot could very easily overstep the flight factor of 2.67g at the maximum design speed above 7000 ft and 2.5g at Mach 0.8.

A two-minute level at maximum power produced 412 mph IAS at 15,800 ft. I could see only two starboard JPT gauges at this point and they showed 650-680 degrees. Then at 220 mph IAS the test pilot cut out the power boost, at my request, and I was able to appreciate that the aircraft could just be flown in that condition in the event of power failure, but with very high control forces.

Finally, I dived the aircraft from 15,000 ft to 4000 ft at maximum cruise power, reaching 500 mph IAS at 5000 ft. Control was still very good at this point, though regular reference to the elevator trimmer had to be made as stick forces increased above 450 mph IAS. Below 5000 ft the air was sufficiently rough to cause considerable wing flexing at this speed, and a six-foot yaw-meter strut on the starboard wing was carrying out the most odd manoeuvres.

I took the aircraft in to the final approach at 150 mph and handed over to the front seat because, as noted before, direct forward view from the rear seat is negligible.

Having sat in the front of seat and seen two landing from the rear, I have the impression that the landing is as straightforward and simple as are all the other flight conditions. Touchdown occurred at 110 mph. The brakes, applied hard, were smooth and powerful in operation and restricted the run to about 1700 yds.

Conclusions

For an aeroplane the equivalent in weight and bomb load to the Lincoln, the B-45 breaks new ground in that its handling qualities compare it more with aircraft in the Mosquito class.

As with the majority of tricycle undercarriage, gas-turbine-powered aircraft, it is simple, even easy, to fly; it has a relatively high Mach number limitation and a remarkable degree of controllability at its design diving speed of 525 mph IAS.

However, as a heavy bomber it has severe limitations with regard to range, height and defensive armament.

The range figures quoted refer to the design operating height of 35,000 ft, but I feel that, even with a reduced bomb load, this is unlikely to be met, and that at full all-up weight this height may well be nearer 28,000 ft, with a consequent reduction in range and operating efficiency. That this is also felt at North American was indicated by statements that much interest is now being centred on the carriage of heavy calibre guns, rockets, and other forms of ground-attack armament for the low-level interdiction role.

It would probably make an excellent strike aircraft as there seemed to be little tendency towards directional instability. It seems highly probable that this will eventually become its role; at low level, making use of speed and weather cover, it could be effective over short ranges whereas, given its relatively low maximum operating height bracket, it lacks the speed, range, and adequate defensive armament to justify its use in the high-level role.

The North American Tornado was a very advanced aeroplane for its time; but it was immediately apparent that if our B3/45 Canberra fulfilled its design potential it would outclass the Tornado, and anything else then under development in the USA, by a handsome margin. It had been a remarkable experience to fly a four-engined jet with such excellent handling qualities so soon after the emergence of the first practical (and much smaller) jet fighters; and there was an even more fascinating experience to come!

Next day, soon after a cold dawn, in the golden early light of the Mojave Desert, a briefing began, again at the North American Flight Test Centre, on the XP-86 'supersonic' research fighter. The briefing officers comprised the Chief Engineer, R. Farren, and the Chief Project Test Pilot, George Welch, and the aircraft to be flown was the second prototype, serial 598.

The briefing was lengthy and thorough, as was appropriate to the importance of the aircraft in the very early days of its development programme — and I was left in no doubt as to the importance of bringing it back without breaking it!

By midday I had absorbed a good knowledge of the test status and systems operation of this interesting aeroplane, and prepared to go out to fly. By now the contrast between the earlier cold dawn, with its mellow sun, and the oven-like Mojave midday glare had become very noticeable.

North American XP-86
General Briefing Data
Sources of information:
Projects Section, USAF, Wright Field.
North American Flight Test Reports:
North American Flight Test Section, Muroc Lake, California — Chief Engineer
 R. Farren,
North American Flight Test Section — Test Pilots G. Krebs, G. Welch.

Design weight gross:	13,453 lb
Design weight empty:	9383 lb
Design useful load:	4070 lb

Dimensions

Span:	31.1 ft
Height:	14.5 ft
Length:	37.5 ft
Wing area:	274 square feet
Dihedral:	Three Degrees
Root chord:	9.9 ft
Tip chord:	63.47 in
Aileron tab (left only):	1.11 square feet
Range:	up seven degrees; down seven degrees
Aileron area:	each 18.6 square feet
Range:	up twenty-five degrees; down eighteen degrees (dynamically balanced about perpendicular axis)
Sweepback:	Thirty-five degrees

The second prototype North American XP86 Sabre, on test over the Mojave desert in 1948, flown by George Welch who had only recently reached Mach 1.0 in it — the first supersonic flight by a fighter aircraft. *(North American)*

Horizontal stabiliser range:	up three degrees; down nine degrees
Taper ratio:	0.513
Aspect ratio:	4.78
Dive brake area:	20.69 feet square (movement seventy degrees)
Mean chord length:	97.03 in
Incidence: root:	+1 degree
tip:	−1 degree
Section: root:	NACA 0012.64 (Modified)
tip:	NACA 0011.64 (Modified)
Max take-off weight:	16,438 lb
Wing loading:	forty-nine pounds per square foot
Power loading:	3.4 lb/lb thrust
Tyre loading:	145 lb (wheels 26 in × 6 ft 6 in main track
Wheelbase:	176.3 in

Performance

Speed (firm's estimate with TG180/3800–4000 lb thrust SLT):	633 mph/16,000 ft
Climb (firm's estimate with TG180/3800–4000 lb thrust SLT):	40,000 ft in 16 mins
Take-off over 50 ft obstacle at 13,3111 lb:	3540 ft
Landing over 50 ft obstacle at 11,845 lb:	2660 ft
Fuel, internal:	435 US gal
Fuel. total (with long-range tanks):	848 US gal
Limiting flight load factors:	-3.00; $+7.33$ (G)

Range

Long-range configuration:	
Max take-off weight:	16,438 lb
Max distance:	1306 miles
Max fuel used:	5680 lb
Max endurance:	3.91 hr
Combat radius with 848 US gal, including thirty minutes' reserve, and thirty minutes at 100 per cent power at operational height:	566 miles at 375 kt/35,000 ft
Service ceiling:	43,500 ft
Stall, slats open, flaps forty degrees, wheels down:	107.8 mph
Cl (max) slats and flaps closed:	0.95 (1.5 at 25 degrees incidence and 1.4 at landing incidence)
Design dive speed:	484 mph IAS 29,000 ft
	640 mph IAS 12,000 ft
	700 mph IAS sea level

TG180 Engine data

Max rating:	4000 lb thrust sea level static (generally accepted as 3800 lb or less)
airflow:	73 lb/sec
rpm:	7600
turbine temp:	1500 degrees F
compressor inlet temp:	59 degrees F

Flight Report on North American second prototype XP-86, serial 598, at Experimental Flight Test Section, North American Aviation, Muroc Lake, California, 21 May 1948

There was no possibility of more than one flight in this aircrat and therefore an attempt had to be made to gain a large amount of information in a short period of time. The following is a description, in chronological order, of the main events of the flight.

Cockpit

During my cockpit check-out I was agreeably surprised with the layout. The windscreen, instrument panel, etc were far nearer to the pilot than is normal American practice. The stick is positioned so that it can be held comfortably with forearm on thigh, another unusual feature. The instrument grouping was reasonably satisfactory in nearly every way.

In general, it gives the feeling of being one with the machine, so essential for the full confidence and therefore efficiency of the pilot, and so often lacking in modern aircraft.

This particular aircraft was fitted with a 'radar reflecting gunsight', mounted below the foot of the front armoured glass panel, and it did not interfere with forward view significantly (TA-1A radar rangefinding GS +AN/APG-5A (M × 215).

The cockpit's pressurisation sealing appeared to be a little primitive, much use being made of a Bostik compound everywhere. The system was not connected and I could not check its operation. North American say they are experiencing very considerable trouble with all aspects of cabin pressurisation, especially in connection with the XB-45. Pressurisation is achieved by airflow from the final stage of the compressor at ten pounds per minute for 'full cool' or fourteen pounds per minute for 'full heat', routed through an after-cooler and a turbine refrigeration pack, or a bypass. Control is by thermostat.

No external de-icing arrangements are made, and internal defrosting of the windscreen and single-skin free-blown hood is by ducted hot air, as mentioned above. It appears that North American have solved the problem, hitherto so acute in fighter circles in the UK, of actually ejecting hot air from a heating system.

Externally the aircraft is well-finished, with the exception of the main intake duct. Inboard of the moulded nose ring, this is a riveted tunnel, the skinning of which appears to be of poor quality.

All aircraft are delivered unpainted, as they say no fillers or paint suitable for use at high speed in rain etc, have been developed yet.

Services

Hydraulics are preferred by North American to electrics, as in their opinion, they are lighter, more flexible and one-tenth the cost. They have no interest in pneumatics. (North American consider that 3000 pounds per square inch pressure is high and troublesome enough for the moment, and they have had some success with aluminium hydraulic cylinders with chromium-plated pistons, dust and dirt being excluded by means of micro-filters).

Take-off

This was made with thirty degrees of flap and slats open. Initially, some difficulty was experienced in lining up for take-off because the nosewheel castoring action was hindered by the crust of the lake bed at slow taxying speeds. Nosewheel steering, which was installed but not connected, will eventually eradicate this.

Acceleration was slow as, with the TG180 engine, the aircraft is underpowered. The nosewheel was lifted at 110 mph and the aircraft flown off smoothly and easily at 140 mph at a sharp angle of attack.

Retracting the undercarriage required considerable trim adjustment nose-down and this was accomplished simply with use of the stick-mounted slide-switch controlling the horizontal stabiliser. The ailerons were very sensitive on take-off and the aircraft could be rocked laterally on the ground with them from 110 mph upwards. Slats were locked in at 350 mph and the climb started at 380 mph IAS. The climb to 35,000 ft at full power (manually controlled to JPT limits) occupied some fifteen minutes, and this was used generally to assess the pilot's position, control, feel etc.

Brief impressions gained were as follows:
Controls are well harmonised. The cockpit layout is quite good. Visibility is good to the side, above and to the rear, but poor forward for a fighter, owing to the heavy structure of windscreen and quarter panel frames.

The aircraft handled excellently, and one did not have any reason to feel that the airframe was other than perfectly orthodox.

At 35,000 ft, 255 mph IAS, the gallons-left counter showed 250 US gal (JPT 700 degrees at maximum power); as it was therefore impracticable to continue to 40,000 ft, as planned, tests were begun from this point.

Speed was increased in a full-power shallow descent to Mach 0.9/29,000 ft where aileron and rudder control were excellent and a ten-pound elevator trim change was in evidence, nose-up. This was held until another reversal occurred, returning trim to neutral at about Mach 0.94, and at Mach 0.97/23,000 ft a further reversal had produced a heavier nose-up moment which was comfortably trimmed out with the stabiliser trimmer.

After zoom-climbing back to about 36,500 ft a steeper maximum power dive was made from 36,000 ft and, according to the Mach meter, unity, or a little over, was reached at 29,000 ft, partially trimmed, with a slight lateral roll in evidence and with some minor buffeting at the tail. The aircraft was perfectly comfortable in this condition.

The drag rise does not make itself really apparent until Mach 0.95–0.96 is reached, at which point the dive angle must be increased considerably for further increase in speed.

Before descending, 3g was pulled at Mach 0.88/30,000 ft and only minor buffeting was felt at this point. A shallow dive was then carried out at Mach 0.85 from 28,000 ft to 10,000 ft, at approximately eighty per cent power. The controls were used vigorously and with fighter manoeuvrability effect at these conditions. The dive brakes, operated by a slide switch on the throttle, were operated during this dive at Mach 0.85/20,000 ft. Reaction was smooth with a ten-to-fifteen pounds nose-up moment, and rapid deceleration.

At 10,000 ft speed was reduced and the machine stalled in the 'clean' configuration, slats locked 'IN'. Stability approaching the stall was of a surprisingly high order; sensitive aileron control remained to the last and after a gentle, but adequate stall warning, buffet beginning at 140–145 mph, the stall occurred at a very steep angle of attack at 131 mph. The right wing tended to drop, but this was held easily and recovery effected in approximately 1200 ft without any attempt to cut things fine. By this time fuel was becoming low and a high indicated speed run was made back to the lake.

During a circuit of the north base at 450–580 mph IAS all controls appeared to be so adequate as to give the impression of flight at a much lower speed and, for this reason, I decided to make a fast run across the high speed course marked on the lake-bed, at least up to the speed at which the temporary anti-spin parachute brackets under the stabiliser should begin to set up buffeting.

As soon as the aircraft was turned onto course at 580 mph and height lost to 3000 ft (above sea level) at full throttle, the aircraft accelerated remarkably quickly in the shallow dive and the ASI soon reached 650 mph (+/− 5 mph in some mild turbulence). Power was reduced and the aircraft eased up out of the rough air at this point, again without any control difficulties other than the necessity to use the horizontal stabiliser actuator as the elevator stick forces were rather high. Then 600 mph IAS was held in a hard turn and through several quarter rolls to assess controllability under these conditions, this was of a very high order indeed.

Fuel shortage made a landing imperative at this point, and this was carried out in a normal 'Spitfire curved approach' manner, keeping power at eighty per cent and speed at 1.4 x stalling until well into the final approach. At this point I remembered that I had not unlocked the slats but, having stalled satisfactorily without them, I continued the approach, touching down easily at 140 mph and, by trimming the stabiliser full 'tail down', held the nosewheel off until 100 mph was reached.

The brakes, applied at ninety mph, were smooth and powerful and were held full-on from seventy mph to standstill without subsequent overheating. There was no tendency to fading and the firm's test pilot says that the brakes, which are multiple disc type, may be used fully from the moment of touchdown without overheating.

Judgement of distance on the dazzling white, dry salt lake was difficult, but on this occasion the landing run, which could have been shortened, was of the order of 1600–1800 yds from touchdown which occurred approximately on the aiming point. The use of slats would have reduced the landing speed by 10 mph or more.

General Notes

The TG 180 suffers from slow acceleration and deceleration and oversensitivity to throttle movement at all altitudes. In all handling characteristics it compares unfavourably with the obsolescent Derwent and Goblin. With its doubtful 4000 lb-thrust SLT the aircraft is at present underpowered.

The overlarge ailerons provide lateral control even during the take-off run, and are inclined to be oversensitive on take-off in the hands of a newcomer. With power boost they provide an exceptional measure of control up to limiting IAS and Mach number. Maximum rates of roll were not measured owing to the X category of the aircraft, but the impression gained was that they would compare with the P-84 (360 degrees/3 sec) at 500 mph, and out-roll it at 600 mph IAS by a fair margin.

Longitudinal trimming by the stick-switch-operated adjustable stabiliser is satisfactory throughout the range of speeds and Mach numbers which I was able to experience. At altitude, at high Mach numbers, it is not too sensitive but provides that rapid trim adjustment which is an essential flight control under such conditions. At lower speeds it is, of course, slower in response but adequate.

At no time in the flight could I detect snaking, though without a gunsight precise assessment of the flight path is difficult.

Apart form the obvious one of the high Mach number/IAS capability, the most significant feature of this aircraft is its ability to manoeuvre operationally at Mach numbers of 0.9 and more, even to the extent of quite high normal accelerations and rates of roll. A further flight to 40,000 ft in this connection to assess accelerated stability would have been of great value, but unfortunately was not possible, as stated earlier.

The cockpit in general is vastly better than those of previous American aircraft. However, there is still room for much imoprovement in the 'sense grouping' field.

Two items rating special mention are: the directly-reflected radar gunsight which obstructs the view forward through the armoured glass panel; and the flap selector lever which operates along a quadrant inboard of the throttle control, calibrated in degrees of flap setting. The lever action is smooth, and the desired flap settings can be selected progressively and instantaneously without the necessity for observation of another indicator.

According to the North American test pilot this feature was very popular, but for some reason unknown to him steps had been taken to provide a different system in production models.

Conclusion
The P-86 is an outstanding aircraft.
1. It can achieve Mach number exceeding unity.
2. Operationally, it is fully controllable at up to Mach 0.97 at least above 20,000 ft, and gives the impression of being even aerobatically controllable at Mach 0.9

It is probably capable of development to an IAS of 700 mph or more. Despite its extremely high performance capabilities, it is an unusually pleasant and straightforward aircraft to fly — possibly more so than most jet fighters from both sides of the Atlantic.

It is not merely a research aircraft, in which field (and that of record-breaking) it is likely to shine, but it is a standard fighter aircraft in production for the USAF who should experience no functional difficulty in operating it.

This flight in the XP-86 was a remarkable experience in 1948 when, without exception, all other jet fighters or even fighter prototypes were still in severe compressibility troubles and limited to strictly subsonic speeds in the range Mach 0.74 to 0.8 with the Vampire, Meteor, Dassault Ouragan (France) and P-80 and P-84 (USA), and, for practical purposes, to little more than Mach 0.9 on all the other swept-wing experimental prototypes of the period.

Significantly, in addition to its breakthrough in aerodynamic performance, the P-86 had all the hallmarks of a classic fighter aeroplane and left one in no doubt of its future as a practical transonic fighter and trend-setter.

Chapter Three
Testing Britain's First Jet Bomber

America's post-war jet experience provided a useful lead into the major test and development programme about to commence in the UK — the English Electric B3/45 twin-engined light jet bomber whose design performance would, if realised, revolutionise military aviation with its potential of target penetration at heights exceeding the capability of all known fighter interception by more than 10,000 ft.

This would also be Britain's first jet bomber, and it seemed set to out-perform all the first jet bombers of the USA and France then under development.

The English Electric A.1 was designed to meet Air Ministry Specification B3 of

The roll-out of Britain's first jet bomber, English Electric's A1, the B3/45 prototype VN 799 at Warton, May 1949. *(British Aerpsoace)*

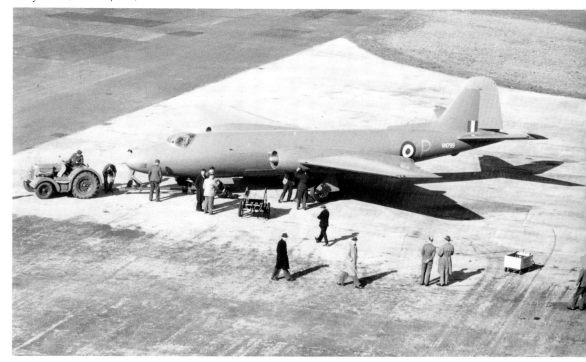

1945 which called for a high altitude bomber capable of carrying a 'Mosquito' bomb load over 1000 miles at not less than 40,000 ft, incorporating a blind-bombing system based on a new and radical radar bomb-sight. This aircraft would take the RAF's bomber force into the jet era.

By 1946 the Chief designer, W. E. W. Petter, and his newly formed design team had decided that the aircraft would be powered by a pair of the newly designed and not yet run Rolls-Royce 'Avon' axial flow, gas turbine engines, each giving initially 6500 lb of thrust; in conjunction with a broad chord, low aspect ratio (4.3) wing, and with a thickness/chord ratio tapered from twelve per cent at the centre section to nine per cent at the tips. This, together with a low wing loading of 40–42 lbs/sq ft, was aimed towards achieving a high-altitude performance, good fuel economy and exceptional manoeuvrability at high and low altitudes and at low speeds.

At Preston the building of the prototype progressed excellently, but by 1947 it had become clear that the new radar bombing system was lagging behind in development and would not be available within the new bomber's planned production timescale (a foretaste of the pattern of airborne radar procurement in this country over the next three decades). So a new specification, B5/47, was issued in November 1947 calling for a tactical day bomber version with a visual bomb aiming system, unarmed and with a crew of three. Performance was to be at least 500 mph at 20,000 ft; range with a 7500 lb bomb load at least 1000 miles, and its service ceiling not less than 40,000 ft.

In fact Petter's classic light jet bomber (soon to be named Canberra in recognition of the first overseas customer — Australia) was to exceed its requirements to a remarkable degree, in that its maximum speed was 600+ mph at the tropopause (approx 36,000 ft); its operating ceiling 47,000 ft; range with bomb-load 1700 miles; and its service ceiling over 50,000 ft (the ultimate version, the PR.9, being cleared to 55,000 ft for service, and reaching 60,000 ft on test).

The English Electric A1 prototype, serial VN 799, airborne for the first time in a short straight 'hop' at Warton in May 1949, flown by the author. *(British Aerospace)*

VN 799 on its first air-photo session, with modified rudder horn balance area, June 1949. *(British Aerospace)*

The prototype of the original B3/45- specification, English Electric A.1, serial VN 799, was test-flown for the first time on 13 May 1949, and was immediately successful as described in the author's report.

The English Electric Co Ltd, Aircraft Division, Warton Aerodrome, Preston.
Experimental Flight Report

Pilot:	R. P. Beamont
Date:	13.5.49
Aircraft type:	B3/45
Aircraft serial No:	VN 799
Flight No:	One
Object of test:	First test flight
Take-off loading:	27,877 lb
Tare weight:	20,337 lb
Fuel (825 gal):	6650 lb
Crew:	200 lb
Bombs, flares, or ballast:	690 lb
Tyre pressures	
Main:	72 lb/sq in
Nose:	60 lb/sq in
C.G. position at take-off:	1.469 ft aft of datum — 19.615 M/C
Time at take-off:	11.46 hr
Time at landing:	12.13 hr
Total flight time:	0.27 hr

Special flight limitations
Aircraft in experimental condition, with 108 lb additional ballast on ballast box.
Fuel distribution:

No. 1 tank	500 gal
No. 2 tank	300 gal
No. 3 tank	25 gal

All services were checked before flight and found satisfactory. Engine figures:

RPM	JPP	OP	OT
7800	600	40	45
7800	620	38	40

Brakes:	main pressure — 440 lb
Tailplane:	1½ divisions from nose down
Isolating switches on	
Power for take-off:	7500/7500
Flaps down time	11.46 — zero

The aircraft was flown off normally at approximately 90 kt and, as the speed exceeded 120 kt IAS, full nose-down trim was insufficient to trim out the subsequent nose-up trim change. At 200 ft, power was reduced and the undercarriage retracted satisfactorily. During this operation a slight yaw to port occurred, a correction for which was made by application of right rudder.

After approximately two inches of travel involving a low control force and a very small rudder reaction, the rudder control lost effectiveness in a manner which suggested over-balance in that control forces were suddenly reduced to zero and no further rudder reaction was noticeable. This condition was corrected rapidly by left rudder pressure and the aircraft climbed straight ahead to approx 5000 ft. Flaps were retracted satisfactorily at 170 kt, after holding the aircraft in trim by a 20–30 lb push force together with full nose-down trim. This resulted in a mild nose-down trim change and the aircraft was trimmed hands off at 245 kt IAS, tailplane 2 graduations up from 'nose-down'.

Right rudder was again applied, this time at 200 kt, with the same results as before, plus the additional impression that, following on the sudden reduction of starboard rudder force to zero, a sharp minus force occurred until held and reversed with port rudder.

During this test it was confirmed that during the over-balance condition a slight tremor could be felt through the rudder system, though not through the airframe.

At this condition of flight (245 kt, 5–6000 ft, time: zero plus three), the tailplane actuator was found to operate satisfactorily, though with some lag, and the aircraft was satisfactorily in trim at a tailplane setting 2 graduations up from full nose-down.

At zero plus eight-and-a-half an ASI check was made with a standard Vampire V with the following results:

B3/45 — 245 kt   Vampire — 245 kt

The Vampire reported all doors and fairings closed.

At zero plus twelve further investigation of the rudder condition was carried out at 210 kt, 6000/6000 RPM, 6–8000 ft, and the condition was confirmed without variation from the previous test, the general impression being that the rudder was effective through very small angles either side of neutral, and over-balanced outside those angles. This condition naturally restricted the scope of the test, but before descending the other controls were checked at this flight condition as follows:

The prototype Canberra shows fine controllability, on test from Warton in 1949. *(British Aerospace)*

Ailerons firm and positive in action with heavy wheel forces for large angles.

Elevator well in harmony with ailerons; positive and firm in action and response. Possibly slightly less positive than ailerons. A slight tremor was noticeable with jerky application which was probably spring-tab effect.

The tailplane actuator was checked at this point and this, though smooth and effective, suffered from an initial lag of between 2–3 seconds between operation of the switch and a noticeable response. This is undesirable, but need not interfere with the early flying.

At zero plus fourteen it was decided that the test should be discontinued owing to the rudder condition which did not promise an adequate measure of control in the single-engine mode, and the descent was begun. During this it was noted that the aircraft lost speed very slowly at idling RPM, and in fact would not do so at any appreciable rate of descent. The flap speed of 140 kt was not reached until zero plus fifteen-and-a-half after a descent from approximately 5000 ft to approximiately 2500 ft, and when flaps were applied the resulting nose-up trim change once again could not be completely trimmed out with tailplane. A normal half circuit was made, the undercarriage being lowered at 120 kt satisfactorily with the warning lights operating within a period of approximately 15 seconds. This did not produce a noticeable trim change.

41

During the crosswind leg and the first part of the final approach at 115–110 kt the aircraft handled easily apart from the rudder condition, control being maintained without the use of rudder; but during the last 1000 yd of the approach at 110 kt IAS, rough air was encountered which set up a series of yaws which could be felt in phase on the rudder but which could not be corrected or controlled by its use; an attempt to do this resulted in recurrence of the over-balance condition.

The hold-off and landing was normal, apart from an excess safety speed, and after cutting the engines 500 yd short of the runway at 100 kt/20 ft, the ASI was still reading 100 kt at the moment of touchdown 7–800 yd further on. The brakes were used quite severely and retarded the aircraft adequately without undue temperature rise.

General Impressions

Apart from the rudder conditions described, the aircraft handled smoothly and easily. All services operated satisfactorily, although in the case of tailplane actuation some alterations may be necessary. Engine behaviour was satisfactory, and no engine handling was carried out owing to the circumstances of the test. Both engines and airframe were remarkably quiet in flight and the noise level in the cockpit allows excellent radio reception.

As was to be expected from the loading condition, the aircraft was stable longitudinally and appeared to be so directionally in smooth air conditions. Rudder and aileron trimmers were set at neutral for take-off and were not required throughout the flight.

During the approach, it was noted that up to its maximum range the tailplane actuator keeps pace with the nose-up trim change caused by flap operation, so that provided the airspeed is kept below 130 kt stick-free trim can be retained during the full operation.

A later Canberra series, the PR7 in 1955, showing the clean aerodynamics which were maintained through all nine major variants. *(British Aerospace)*

Work Before Next Flight
1. Inspect brake assemblies and check Thermo-couples.
2. Remove flap system stop for full travel.
3. Mark tailplane dial graduations 0–9 (to suit), top to bottom.
4. Investigate rudder control.

Rapid progress was made in the next three months of flight testing, and in initial exploration of a large part of the design flight envelope the handling qualities were found to be exceptional. This resulted in thenew jet bomber being entered for the SBAC Display in September where, at its public debut, it gave a show of aerobatics which was considered remarkable for a bomber aircraft and astonished world aviation.

Flight testing continued with increasing success, and in early 1950 the first of two B5/47 production standard Canberra B Mk 2s, WD 932, was cleared by the Company for acceptance trials in the USA. For these tests the full compressibility envelope had been established and plotted as a curve of advisory 'never exceed' Mach limitations for the Martin Company and USAF test pilots.

The plotted points indicated the assessed limits of safe control, and the limiting conditions varied from severe 'eight-cycle' longitudinal airframe oscillations (incipient elevator flutter coupling with airframe natural frequency) at the points from low altitude to 10,000 ft; on through heavy roughness and buffeting from Mach 0.8 at 20,000 ft, and then left wing heaviness and powerful nose-up trim change with violent buffet at Mach 0.84–0.85 at 20,000 ft and above. After this, at beyond Mach 0.86, if the pilot was very determined the nose-up out-of-trim force changed sharply to nose-down while still in violent buffet (see Heinrich Beauvais' experience, page 8) and recovery from the consequent steep dive, even with immediate full-back pull force, was dramatically slow.

For all future Canberra flying, Mach 0.86 was defined as the 'never-exceed' compressibility limit at 20,000 ft and above; but on one occasion production test pilot J. W. C. Squier inadvertently exceeded the Mach 0.86 limit, encountered the violent pitch-down and was unable to recover from the resulting nearly vertical dive until after a height loss of more than 15,000 ft and reaching approximately Mach 0.9 in the process. Various parts of the airframe were over-stressed, and this was a further classic example of loss of control in compressibility.

In the early 1950s military aviation had still not achieved a significant performance increase, and would not do so until this positive barrier to progress could be penetrated with confidence and in full conventional control.

In the USA, the late 1940s' crop of jet bomber and fighter prototypes still under development in 1950, continued to encounter this barrier, bombers at Mach 0.75–0.78 and fighters at Mach 0.8–0.84, with one exception. This was the F-86 Sabre which was about to enter service as the first military airplane in the world with clearance to, and adequate control at, Mach 1.0 — the speed of sound!

In the UK the post-war line of jet fighter developments had resulted in the beautiful Hawker Hunter, soon to become a classic transonic fighter but, in 1950, still some way from squadron service.

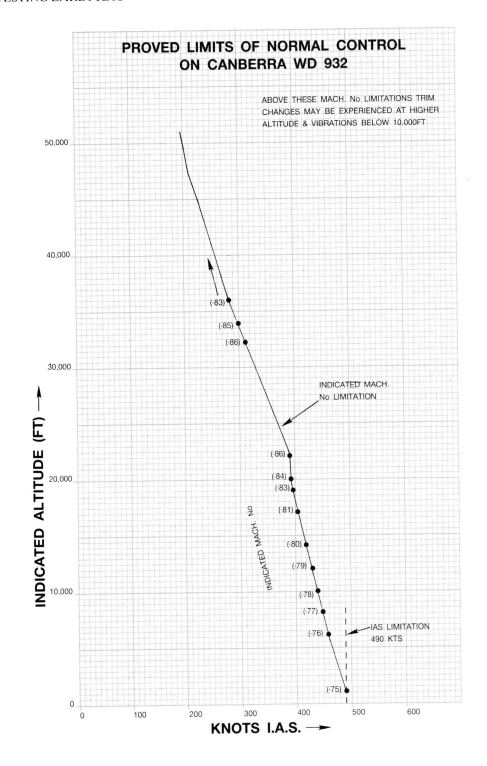

PROVED LIMITS OF NORMAL CONTROL
ON CANBERRA WD 932

ABOVE THESE MACH. No LIMITATIONS TRIM
CHANGES MAY BE EXPERIENCED AT HIGHER
ALTITUDE & VIBRATIONS BELOW 10,000FT

INDICATED MACH.
No LIMITATION

INDICATED ALTITUDE (FT)

INDICATED MACH. No

IAS LIMITATION
490 KTS

KNOTS I.A.S.

After entering squadron service in 1951 (No. 101 Squadron Binbrook), the Canberra was able to evade all fighter interceptions for a number of years merely by operating at heights well beyond their reach, and this caused so much embarrassment during the Annual Defence exercises over the North Sea that from 1953 onwards the Canberra force was actually required to operate down at altitudes 'more suitable' to the Meteor and Hunter defence force; but even then the speed of the attacking Canberras and their manoeuvrability resulted in embarrassingly few interceptions!

So the scene was very clearly set: It was essential that the next generation of interceptor fighters have supersonic performance with practical combat manoeuvrability at these speeds.

The first Canberra, VN799, on the flight-line at Warton in early 1950, together with the three other prototypes. *(British Aerospace)*

The flight development of the Canberra in all its variants continued for over a decade, and there were many interesting and some exciting experiences.

A test sortie that produced an example of the unexpected, for which the experimental test pilot must always be prepared, occurred on 7 February 1950 at Warton, the English Electric Company test airfield in Lancashire. It was a day of crisp, clear visibility below the fair weather cumulus clouds of a small ridge of high pressure which was expected to last for the rest of the day — a day in fact for pressing on with the Canberra development programme which had been gaining momentum at an impressive rate ever since the prototype first flight nine months before on Friday 13 May 1949.

In that period four B1 prototypes, VN799, VN813, VN828 and VN850, had all flown successfully and reliably, and with so few mechanical or aerodynamic problems that excellent progress had been made in exploring and expanding the flight envelope into the compressibility range beyond Mach 0.85, and to above 50,000 ft and the Vne design limit of 500 kt IAS.

45

The Canberra was already regarded as something of a phenomenon in the aviation world, but at Warton there was a strong consciousness that despite all this early success there remained a massive programme of flight and ground testing to prove this radical new jet bomber to the standard of CA Release into service with the RAF.

This was being tackled with dedication and enthusiasm at all levels in the factory, in the teams led by Ray Creasey (aerodynamics), Don Crowe (engineering), Dai Ellis (flight development), and in all the other experimental and production disciplines at Warton, Preston and Samlesbury under the overall design leadership of W. E. W. Petter and the production management of Arthur Sheffield.

As chief test pilot it was my good fortune (and, of course, duty) to carry out the first-time exploratory testing of all new designs. This had resulted in personal experience of over 100 hours of Canberra prototype testing by February 1950, and as I prepared to take the next flight on the first prototype B1, VN799, still resplendent in its 'Petter blue' paintwork, but with the rudder horn-balance area reduced since flight one, it was with the comfortable confidence that this would be yet another thoroughly enjoyable and interesting flight in a quite superb aeroplane.

The test schedule, which like all the others I had discussed and agreed with the flight test engineers before clearing it for issue, called for a maximum rate, full power climb at the moderate weight of full internal fuel but no ballast to represent bomb-load; the intention being to clear engine and systems suitability in this 'outside the norm' fast climb performance condition.

There had been no reason to suppose from all previous lower climb-rate, maximum continuous engine power climbs, that any critical areas might be encountered.

Then, after completing the climb to 40,000 ft in about ten minutes (depending on the temperature and height of the Tropopause), there would be some further investigation of limiting Mach No, through the initial compressibility buffeting around 0.83, to an expected Mach 0.86 at 30,000 ft where a powerful nose-up pitch was anticipated.

It promised to be an interesting and uncomplicated flight, and in the prevailing lovely weather over the Irish Sea and the Lake District, likely to be most enjoyable.

The walk down the 'tarmac' from Flight operations to where the familiar blue shape was waiting was pleasantly refreshing after the stuffy meeting I had just left. After the usual pre-flight checks and a few words with the ever-cheerful ground-staff foreman, Jimmy Pickthall, and his ground crew who regarded the Canberra proudly as 'their aircraft', which indeed it was, I ducked under the low entrance door to avoid a glancing blow from its sharp edge which had drawn blood on occasions before, (all military aircraft cockpits seem to carry risk of injury to the occupants, at least until eventual modification can be made!) and climbed up into the familiar Martin Baker Mk. 1 ejection seat under the single-piece 'blown' Perspex canopy which gives the Canberra its unique pilot view.

When flying a T4 Canberra forty years later, most kindly provided by RAF Wyton on the occasion of their splendid 40th Anniversary of the Canberra reunion celebration, and captained by S/Ldr Dave Watson, the longest serving Canberra QFI with thirty-six years on type, I was impressed with the painstaking deliberations of the pre-flight checks and procedures which have resulted from the laudable and dedicated concentration of the Service on flight safety. Yet on looking back to 1950 I wondered if our procedures on Canberra then had been less safe — they certainly took much less than half the time to complete!

Starting up this, for the time, very high performance aircraft was simplicity itself. Parachute and seat harness on. Oxygen and emergency oxygen connected and tested. R/T plugged in and checked with Tower. Seat height adjusted. D.V. panel open for any checks with ground crew. Cockpit door closed and locked. HP fuel cocks on. LP fuel on. Throttles closed. Battery Master on. Generators on. Forward, Mid and Aft fuel tank pumps on. Brakes on.

Signal ground crew for start up. Port starter switch on and press button. Fire up and confirm reaching Idle speed without exceeding jet pipe temperature limits.

Repeat for starboard engine. Check flap operation. Three way visual control checks and airbrake checks with ground crew, then R/T taxy clearance and 'chocks away'.

It hardly took longer than it takes to read it. There were other checks to be completed while taxying and at the run-up point, but the whole procedure from closing the door to beginning the take-off roll would seldom take longer than fifteen minutes, often less, and I cannot recall any in-flight incident on our Canberras that resulted from ommission in pre-flight checks.

For this flight the normal fuel tank procedure would be followed, namely all tanks on for take-off and then switch off 1 and 2 to maintain forward CG during the climb and until the indicated fuel level in No 3 (aft tank) dropped to 800 lbs, after which all tanks on again and monitored to maintain the required CG.

So, at the end of the westerly runway on the 26 numbers, the Avon RA2s of VN799 were brought up to take-off power against the powerful Dunlop brakes: 'You are clear to take-off and climb initially on 260' from the Tower and, with brake lever released, 799 began its familiar but always satisfying, smooth and powerful acceleration with rudder directional control taking over comfortably from differential braking at about 60 kt.

Wheel eased back progressively from 80 kt brought the nosewheel smoothly off at 95 and unstick at 110. Then wheel forward to hold shallow climb as the undercarriage retracted. At the 150 kt single-engine safety speed, climb angle increased slightly and held until 350 kt, which would be maintained for this sortie at full power until intersecting Mach 0.7 which was the climb datum to 40,000 ft.

Passing 5000 ft over the Ribble estuary, with clearing skies over the sea the Lancashire coastline spread out ahead; Southport, Liverpool, the Wirral, and on to Colwyn Bay. The Great Orme, Snowdonia and Anglesey; and now turning in the climb gently to starboard, Blackpool, Barrow, St Bee's Head and the Lake District mountains, and in the west the Isle of Man and Douglas.

It was always good to fly in these skies in one of the world's finest aircraft.

The cockpit of VN799 was, as usual, smooth, quiet and comfortable, and the climb path was maintained with finger-tip control, the Canberra's stability and dead-beat damping in pitch and roll ensuring an undeviating flight path with minimal attention from the pilot, almost as if it were on auto-pilot.

A radio call to Warton confirming height and heading, 15,000 ft and 310 degrees, and then a subtle change. The cause was not immediately apparent — all systems readings normal, engines sounding healthy, climb performance good. Yet there was something different.

Trim was checked, first in pitch and the elevator response was normal; then in yaw, and while the rudder response was normal, correcting the resulting rolling moment due to yaw with ailerons showed immediately where a problem was arising. The aeroplane did not respond to aileron correction.

This changed the priorities. Power was reduced and the climb levelled at 18,000 ft, and half aileron either way produced heavy wheel forces but no roll response at all; but when full wheel was applied to the right there was a gritty grinding sensation followed by a slow bank to starboard. The ailerons had moved but were clearly restricted; and now they did not centre when the wheel-force was released, and a heavy centring force was needed to trim back to wings level.

The same thing occurred with left wheel force, and this began to suggest obstruction by a foreign object anywhere between the control column gears, through the push-rod and bell crank bearings to the aileron and tab torque tubes.

There was no immediate emergency as level flight could be controlled adequately without ailerons, although heading changing by rudder alone would have limitations in fine control and there might be landing problems — but that could wait.

The next step was to repeat full aileron either way, and with a maximum two handed force to the right no grating movement occurred this time, but then slowly the aircraft began to roll to port, i.e. in the wrong direction! This gave a clue and full left wheel also produced a slow roll response, to starboard.

Clearly the aileron circuit was jammed somewhere, but as the wound-up torque tubes were still operating the 'spring' tabs correctly in the absence of aileron movement (causing the opposite roll response), it now seemed likely that the ailerons only were jammed and not the control circuit to them.

The possibility remained of jamming by a foreign object, but there were two other probable causes, icing up or mechanical jamming by differential expansion or contraction somewhere due to higher than usual rate of climb into the low temperature at altitude.

With this thought in mind I began a slow descent, checking the ailerons both ways at 500 ft intervals. They remained firmly jammed at first, and then suddenly partially freed with grating jerks at around 15,000 ft. This was encouraging, and finally at 11,000 ft the jerkiness, stiffness and lack of response disappeared, and full normal aileron control returned.

In this period of considerable preoccupation I had not radioed an emergency call, and now one was not necessary although the return to base would have to be made with the possibility of a recurrence of the problem in mind.

But first to eliminate another unknown. If it was a distortion caused by low temperature it should be repeatable; so after turning on to a southerly heading over Windermere for the recovery to Warton, I opened up to climb power and began to check the ailerons each way at intervals on the climb. All was normal until at around 15,000 ft the aileron control began to stiffen up, and then at 17,000 ft it became grating and jerky, and finally locked solid again around 19,000 ft; and again forceful use of the wheel produced slow opposite-sense roll response.

All these conditions disappeared again when descending below 12,000 ft, and this was proof positive. I now knew what was happening and already had a good idea of 'why'.

At this point a call to Warton was made for a priority descent west of the field clear of cloud over the sea, and with this established 799 was taken well down-wind to line up for a long precautionary approach which would make little demand on lateral control.

A smooth, steady approach, a normal flare and the customary Canberra easy touchdown, and another experimental sortie in this fascinating programme was over. But this one had been unusual in having produced an interesting and potentially serious defect.

Taxying off the Main and up the short SE-NW runway, I turned into the bay at the west end of Warton's long tarmac, completed the shut-down checks and switched off. Only 35 minutes had elapsed since take-off but it seemed very much longer.

As the cockpit door was opened by the ground staff, letting in a refreshing blast of cold air, I asked Jimmy Pickthall to open the bottom shrouds of both ailerons and there, on both sides, score marks could be seen where the aileron balancing 'beaks' appeared to have 'picked up' on the forward shrouds.

This was confirmed in the subsequent investigation and it was temporarily fixed by local increase of the shroud gaps, but the problem recurred in production Canberras at Samlesbury and some revisions were necessary to the production build standard to eliminate the problem.

It has been an interesting occurrence, and was one of the few serious defects encountered in the development of this remarkable aeroplane.

Frequently Canberra testing involved record times-over-distance. Sometimes they were officially recorded as World Records, and one of these involved the prototype Canberra Mk. V VX185 which began its flight trials with uprated Rolls Royce RA7 engines (Avon Mk 109) giving 7500 lbs SLST, on 15 July 1952, at the English Electric test airfield, Warton, in Lancashire.

This was the fifth development of the B3/45 series to fly in the three years since the first flight of the first prototype B1, serial VN799, on Friday 13 May 1949; the others being the B Mk 2, PR3 and T4 trainer — a remarkable rate of progress in what was already becoming widely recognised as an exceptionally successful programme.

The Mk V specification was for a long-range target-maker and it incorporated a number of significant design changes, including increased fuel capacity in integral wing leading-edge tanks (the first wing tankage in Canberra series) and the uprated RR Avon RA7 engines, each giving 7500 lbs SSLT.

Dunlop Maxaret brakes were a standard fit and there was provision in the weapons bay for extra fuel tankage as an alternative fit.

As with the previous prototypes, a high rate of test flying was soon achieved, with

Canberra Mk V prototype, VX185, taking off from Aldergrove at the beginning of its record crossing of the Atlantic twice in one day. *(British Aerospace)*

emphasis on the new fuel system which soon showed up a problem area associated with extended cruising in the −55°C or less temperatures at the tropopause.

Fuel pressue warning lights came on, and ultimately engine flame-outs occurred when flying on the new wing tanks only. This was caused by fuel-waxing in these conditions and had been predicted.

Once the exact conditions had been established in a number of flights, the matter was referred to the fuel companies in the expectation that an additive could be developed long-term to prevent waxing. Meanwhile, the flight test programme was not delayed as the fuel drill was changed to using the wing-tank fuel first on the climb and initial cruise, and switching to the fuselage (non-critical) tankage before waxing could occur.

Range-proving was critical for this long-range operation and 3½–5 hour cruise-climbs from the top of the initial climb at the tropopause soon became the order of the day at Warton.

Initially these were carried out around the coastline of the British Isles, but at Canberra speeds (Mach 0.72 to Mach 0.8, depending on the schedule) it often became necessary to 'go round again', and so the pattern was varied to taking the first leg out to Ocean Station *Jig* — the Atlantic weather ship approximately 500 nms west of Shannon — before turning eastbound up the Channel to Dover and then on up the North Sea to Orkney.

These cruise-climbs terminated at 48–50,000 ft and at that height were entirely free of any conflicting traffic and rather boring; but on one occasion when in-bound over Southern Ireland on 21 August (as I recollect it without overflying authority, in the rather informal circumstances of those days!) we had had a towering 'anvil' storm cloud in sight in the south for over an hour, and as we approched Cornwall this monstrous development towered well above our height of 45,000 ft.

Just before penetrating it, the lower layers could be seen to glow with continuous lightning and the bottom layers seemed to be of an ominously dark sulphurous haze.

At about this time we received met. warnings of heavy storm activity and an expected jet-stream and turbulence at our level, both of which were already much in evidence, and after some quite violent IF we broke out of the east side of the 'anvil' into clear air over Portsmouth and continued on our way back to base via Cape Wrath in Sutherland.

On landing at Warton, reports were coming in of a flood disaster in Devon and we had in fact just flown through the top of the Lynmouth disaster storm at its height.

During this work two things became apparent: firstly, that the Mk. V was yet another successful Canberra variant and, secondly, that more relevant data could be obtained on its SFC (specific fuel consumption) by long straight sectors rather than by continuing round and round the British Isles; so plans were made to send a small servicing team to Gander, Newfoundland, and to set up final range proving flights to and from there across the North Atlantic.

As this was being worked up, it also became apparent that with 4½ hours average for the 1800 nms approximate sectors, and with our own turn-round team at Gander, the outer and return flights could quite reasonably be done on the same day in an elapsed time of about ten hours if all went well. This was proposed and, after the predictable uproar about 'unnecessary risk to a valuable prototype' from the equally predictable negative thinkers, a more positive appreciation was achieved and the flight was on!

But we had not anticipated the media 'hype' which followed. The Royal Aero Club were to monitor these flights for 'record' purposes, and it at once became widely splurged as 'The First Double Atlantic'! Nevertheless, as it was important to obtain the maximum technical value from the operation, this was given the formal priority, to the indignant astonishment of some media men who found it unbelievable that the take-off and return landing times would be based on operational necessity for this 'experimental' category test flight, and not on their copy dead-lines!

So on 25 August 1952, VX185 was positioned at RAF Aldergrove near Belfast for departure, if conditions were suitable, on the following day — the Royal Aero Club having insisted that the sectors must for record purposes be seen as capital city to capital city flights, and ruling against our proposition that for this purpose Preston was the undoubted 'capital' of the North-West!

A met. briefing indicated marginally adequate conditions for the next day and, at a final review at 4 a.m. on 25 August the decision was made to accept what now seemed likely to be a near-limiting headwind for the outbound leg.

VX185 was glistening with moisture in the damp dawn as the crew, the author (captain), Peter Hillwood (co-pilot to fly the return leg) and Dennis Watson (navigator) climbed aboard and began the pre-start checks. This was going to be an interesting day.

The following extracts from English Electric Company Ltd Experimental Flight Report, Canberra B22/48 serial VX185, describe the events:

The English Electric Co. Ltd.
Aircraft Division, Warton Aerodrome, Preston.
Experimental Flight Report

Flight No:	121
Date:	26 August 1952
Aircraft type:	Canberra B22/48
serial no.:	VX.185
Object of test:	Atlantic crossing Aldergrove to Gander.
Pilot:	R. P. Beamont/P. Hillwood
Navigator:	D. A. Watson

Take-off loading

Tare weight:	22,511
Fuel:	23,672
Miscellaneous (stowage boxes and personal equipment	500
Crew	672
Total	47,355 lb
Fuel:	
No. 1 Tank	520 galls
No. 2 tank	317 galls
No. 3 tank	550 galls
Integral Tanks	900 galls
Bomb Bay Tank	650 galls
Tyre Pressures	
Main:	130 lb/sq in
Nose:	104 lb/sq in
Oleo Pressures	
Main:	550 lb/sq in
Nose:	1500 lb/sq in
C.G. position at take off	
2.655' aft of datum	27.47% S.M.C.
Time at take-off:	06.34
Time at landing:	11.12
Total:	04.38
Point to point time:	04.34
Special flight limitations	Nil

Summary

Canberra Mk. V, No. VX185, was flown from Aldergrove, Northern Ireland, to Gander, Newfoundland, and return to Aldergrove in an elapsed time of 10 hours 4 minutes on 26 August 1952.

In general the operating conditions of this exercise were satisfactory from the points of view of control and serviceability, and of seat comfort, and the crew suffered little fatigue after it. However, cockpit heating was found to be inadequate for operation under these conditions, and the inference is that it would be even less adequate for full night operation. It is not considered feasible that extra clothing should be worn, and attention must be given, therefore, to improving considerably cockpit heating arrangements in order to make night operation as comfortable for the crew as day operation, as it is only with reasonable comfort that maximum crew efficiency can be obtained.

The scale of navigational equipment carried proved adequate for the return section of the flight, but inadequate for the outward section owing to ineffectiveness of the Loran installation.

Introduction

VX185 was fitted with Rolls Royce RA.7 Avons as a trial installation during June. The first flight was made on 15 July 1952, and a series of handling, development flights, and long-range proving flights were carried out in July and August.

It was intended to carry out a return flight from Aldergrove to Gander and back to Aldergrove as the culminating point of these trials, and ground facilities were positioned in Ireland and Newfoundland from August 20 for this purpose.

Arrangements were made for the most accurate meteorological forecasting facilities to be available, and for constant watches to be kept by weather ships *Jig* and *Coca*, which were to be alerted by Prestwick from one hour before take-off.

The flight was planned to be carried out by normal navigational methods, cross-checked with information available from the equipment carried which consisted of 20 channel VHF, Marconi ADF, and Loran.

During final tests some difficulty was experienced in obtaining consistent results with Loran owing to recurrent inverter failures, and unsteady voltage delivery, and to suspect aerial deficiency. However, as the ADF had given consistent results, it was decided to regard Loran as a possible alternative rather than a main navigational aid.

The aircraft was flown to Aldergrove on the afternoon of 25 August, and later that afternoon a close study of the Atlantic weather situation with the Air Ministry forecaster indicated that landing conditions at Gander for the following day and at Aldergrove later in the day, were likely to be suitable. A system lay over the route which gave promise of consistent headwinds in the neighbourhood of 40,000 ft, reaching as high as 60–70 kt dead ahead in the neighbourhood of latitude 50. Further outlook for the next three days did not seem promising, and as it was known that by cruising at higher IMN, some 20 kt TAS could be gained in I.C.A.N. conditions over the previous westerly flight in WD940, it was felt that a wind component of up to 55 kt would still allow the possibility of beating the existing westerly time. On this basis therefore, coupled with the fact that the return flight conditions were likely to be favourable, a provisional decision was taken for take-off at 6.30 a.m. B.S.T. on the following morning.

At 4 a.m. B.S.T. the forecaster had a changed picture to describe and while the Gander landing weather forecast remained favourable with little or no low cloud, a jet stream had developed overnight in the area of latitude 50, while the ridge previously lying off N.W. Ireland had straightened out in such a way as to indicate almost continuous headwinds throughout the flight. Wind speeds of 100 kt had been measured in the Irish coastal area at 40,000 ft, while in the area of the jet stream they were reported as high as 140 kt. The long-range forecast still indicated a general deterioriation in landing conditions for the next three days which were, of course, critical to this operation, and therefore a close study was made of the possibilities of evading, or at least reducing, the effect of these very high headwinds at 40,000 ft. The tropopause was reported to be at 41,000 ft, and it became clear that an initial climb to, and thereafter a constant gain in height above the tropopause could result in an effective reduction in headwinds of the order of 5 kt per thousand ft, and it was decided therefore, to abandon the previous intention to cruise at constant height and the highest possible cruising Mach number and to substitute for this a technique aimed at combining an adequate cruising Mach number with absolute cruising ceiling throughout the flight.

Aldergrove–Gander

The decision was taken therefore, to take off as near to the provisional E.T.D. as possible, having regard to the time lost during these unexpected deliberations, and after some difficulty in clearing the canopy of external dew in the cold and very humid dawn, take-off occurred at 6.34 B.S.T. and course was set at 6.35 B.S.T. after a timing run across the airfield.

The climb technique employed was to use 400 kt IAS until this coincided with 0.76 IMN, and then to maintain 0.76 IMN constant at climbing power until the estimated weight/0.76 cruising ceiling had been exceeded. The cruise was commonced after a slight dive, therefore, at 42,700 ft at 0.76/212 with the following fuel conditions:

Integrals	275/265
Mains	480/280/510
Belly	650

IMN was maintained at 0.76 and concentration ws given to keeping the aircraft at its absolute weight ceiling for this Mach number. For this purpose maximum permissible engine conditions were used, and at the end of each hour combat power was applied for the limiting period. This resulted in a small height gain above the cruise ceiling in each case, and when power was reduced to cruising at the end of the limiting period, IMN was kept constant by the necessary small loss of height. In no case did this loss of height exceed 50 per cent of the gain in height obtained by full power.

VHF radios were tested during the climb and when working Scottish centre were both found to be serviceable. Some difficulty was encountered in identifying the beacon on weather ship *Jig*, and it was finally concluded that, owing to the short signals received from this ship, it was not operating a constant watch. Weather ship *Jig* was heard on VHF, but could not be contacted although the aircraft passed within approximately 150 miles of the ship's position.

At 7.46 B.S.T. 45,000 ft had been reached, and IMN were increased to 0.775/200 kt. The flight, which had been carried out up to this point with integral tanks only, was continued with No. 3 tank ON and wing tanks showing 100/100 gallons. Throughout the flight the fuel drill standardised during proving flights was employed, and functioned entirely satisfactorily, i.e. take-off all tanks ON, climb — integral tanks ON only and cruise until 100 gallons indicated. Continue cruise on No. 3 and integrals until No. 3 indicated 300 gallons. Transfer from belly until No. 3 full. Switch off integrals when indicating 25 gallons. Continue on No. 3 transferring from belly at intervals until belly contains approximately 100 gallons. Final hour on all main tanks.

At 8.33 B.S.T. 46,000 ft was reached at 0.77/193, and it was decided to continue the climb to 47.000 ft, and to hold that height while Mach number built up as far as possible.

Navigational information from weather ship *Jig* having been scanty, considerable emphasis was placed on attempting to obtain a known position from American weather ship *Coca*. Again the beacon was only picked up for short periods, and this gave the impression that the radio compass was unserviceable, or that the beacon was not on constant watch; and once again, although the weather ship could be heard transmitting on VHF, two-way communication could not be obtained with either aircraft set, although the aircraft passed within 90 miles of the ship's position. During this period a number of airline and transport aircraft could be heard attempting to work the weather ship on VHF, all without success and eventually two-way communication was established with a trans-Canada airliner which said it believed the American weather ship's VHF receiver was unserviceable. No radar fix was available at this point therefore and with the scanty information obtained from brief ADF bearings, the forecast winds were only roughly confirmed and it was hoped that a reliable known position would be obtained by running fix from St Johns, Newfoundland. It was anticipated that this would be raised at upwards of 500 miles, and although this was in fact the case, again only a five minute signal was obtained before this station apparently went off the air.

The flight had been carried out over cloud tops reaching to 38,000–40,000 ft, and at the approximate let-down point of 200 nautical miles from Gander, this high cloud dispersed as forecast, leaving ⅞ st.cu. at approximately 4000 ft. No further help could be obtained from St Johns, and therefore no further navigation aids could be expected until Gander range could be picked up at 80 miles, and finally Gander VHF, G.C.A., at approximately 40 miles. The navigator, who had up to this point obtained only the scantiest information, was now of the opinion that the aircraft was likely to be approximately 40 miles north of track, and for this reason a five degree course alteration was made to port, and the let-down was begun.

During the previous half hour the aircraft had been kept at 0.8 IMN, and this was now increased progressively until 0.85 was reached at 40,000 ft. This was continued on a shallow descent until at 30,000 ft breaks could be seen in the cloud sheet ahead and eventually land was sighted on the port bow at a range of approximately 100 miles. Soon after this Fogo Island was identified dead ahead, and confirmed the suspected track error of approximately 40 miles north. The necessary course alteration was made to port to line up with Gander, and the latter was raised on VHF at approximately 100 miles at 28,000 ft.

On let-down a fixed throttle (6800 rpm) surge of the type previously encountered on test was experienced on both engines simultaneously at 25,000 ft/340 kt.

The descent was continued at 90 per cent airframe limits, until Gander was sighted and crossed at 1,000 ft prior to lining up with Gander Lake and flying over the timing point at 300 ft.

The landing was made without delay and the aircraft handed over to the servicing party, the only unserviceable item to be rectified being the instrument emergency supply torque switch. A ground check was called for on both VHF radios and the ADF, which were all found to be serviceable. No further checks were called for on the Loran installation.

Take-off Aldergrove:	0.634 B.S.T.
Landing Gander:	11.12 B.S.T.
Observed time point to point:	4 hours 34 minutes
Distance:	1818 nautical miles

Meteorological and airfield clearance was obtained while servicing was in progress for the return flight to Aldergrove, and while some deterioration was forecast for the landing weather at Aldergrove, it did appear that providing the aircraft returned by 1700 hours B.S.T. at the latest, the landing weather would be satisfactory. The outward leg had confirmed the speeds of the forecast winds, and at the same time the Atlantic forecaster at Gander was able to indicate a further straightening out of the ridge off N.W. Ireland, which in itself indicated even more favourable winds for the return journey. Therefore, while the co-pilot and navigator were resting and taking refreshment, a flight plan was filed involving a climb to 41,000 ft, followed by a constant cruise at 41,000 ft in the peak of the tail winds, with a constant reduction of power with reduction of weight, giving an estimated flying time of 3 hours 30 minutes from Gander to Aldergrove.

Owing to the speed of the turn-round of the ground party, the aircraft was ready before the navigation plan had been finalized, and the navigator finished this between take-off and the top of the climb.

The descent to Gander Lake had been carried out at Mach 0.84 until intersecting 500 KIAS and holding this (in the characteristic heavy 'eight cycle' compressibility buffet) until identifying the Royal Aero Club official observer (in his launch on the Lake) and overflying him fast and low for his time check.

During this phase Watson and I had resumed and tightened our top harness straps (after using the lap straps only for comfort purposes for the main portion of the flight), but Peter Hillwood had come forward from his ejection seat at the back to sit on the jump-seat by the pilot to help in the map-reading run-in to Gander Lake. He subsequently described the Mach 0.84 ride in compressibility without seat harness as 'quite interesting'!

After four hours over 8/8ths, the sudden breaking into the endless visibility over Newfoundland's rocky coasts and hills, pine forests and brilliant blue lakes and rivers was a startling contrast, and for a moment there was worry about 'where is the airport' as I turned the Canberra, still at over 450 kt with the throttles closed, on to the new heading; but as I called the airport for joining instructions there ahead at only a few miles beyond a low range of fir-clad hills stretched the white runways of Gander International.

A tight down-wind and base pattern, and then curving in to Finals for touch-down 'on the numbers' and quick turn off and taxy to the main apron where the English Electric ground support team in smart white overalls headed by John Crowther, swarmed upon VX185 as if it was just another sortie at Warton.

With no immediate technical defects the turnround was complete before the rest of the formalities, and as we climbed aboard for the return leg Watson had not had time to finish his navigation plan, which he then proceeded to do during the climb on the first heading.

The Gander Met. office briefing coupled with our outbound experience of the Atlantic weather suggested that we would benefit from a 100 kt jet-stream tailwind virtually all the way across if we stayed at around 41,000 ft, just below the tropopause, and that a warm front had moved into the Aldergrove area as predicted and would result in low cloud and rain on our estimated ETA, but within our operation minima.

So that was decided. We would make a fast climb on course, levelling at 41,000 ft and reducing to maximum continuous power. Then, holding this height, power would be reduced as necessary with fuel burn to maintain firstly Mach 0.79 until an adequate fuel margin was assured to permit speed to be increased over the last hour to Mach 0.81. This would be converted to 500 KIAS on the descent and would be maintained until over-flying the official observer at Aldergrove. This would of course depend on full serviceability, good navigational accuracy and the degree of help obtainable from the various facilities in Ulster.

The progress of the flight was recounted in the following extracts from the Flight Report:

The English Electric Co. Ltd.
Aircraft Division, Warton Aerodrome, Preston.
Experimental Flight Report

Flight No:	122
Date:	26 August 1952
Aircraft type:	Canberra B22/48
serial no.:	VX.185
Object of test:	Atlantic crossing Gander to Aldergrove.
Pilot:	P. Hillwood/R. P. Beamont
Navigator:	D. A. Watson

Take-off loading

Tare weight:	22,511
Fuel:	23,672
Miscellaneous (stowage boxes and personal equipment	500
Crew	672
Total	47,355 lb
Fuel:	
No. 1 Tank	520 galls
No. 2 tank	317 galls
No. 3 tank	550 galls
Integral Tanks	900 galls
Bomb Bay Tank	650 galls
Tyre Pressures	
Main:	130 lb/sq in
Nose:	104 lb/sq in
Oleo Pressures	
Main:	550 lb/sq in
Nose:	1500 lb/sq in
C.G. position at take off	
2.655' aft of datum	27.47% S.M.C.
Time at take-off:	13.10
Time at landing:	16.39
Total:	03.29
Point to point time:	03.26
Special flight limitations	Nil

Gander–Aldergrove

The aircraft was flown over the timing point on Gander Lake after take-off, and course was set at 13.14 B.S.T. with the aircraft being climbed to altitude at climbing power. 41,200 ft was reached at 14.00 B.S.T., and the cruise was begun at 0.79/229.

Fuel handling throughout the flight was carried out as before, and recourse to limiting periods of full power in every hour was not necessary. At the end of the first hour power was reduced to 7150/7150 to maintain 0.8 IMN.

During ground checking it has been found that the radio compass installation was serviceable, and that St Johns radio station had gone off the air for half and hour during the period in which use was being made of it on the outward crossing. This was now obtained full strength, as was the beacon from weather ship *Coca*. Soon after take-off weather ship *Coca* could be heard calling the Canberra on VHF, and these transmissions were eventually very loud and clear at ranges of up to approximately 350 miles. At no time were VX185's transmissions heard apparently on *Coca*, and once again this ship was passed without obtaining two-way contact. ADF bearings from the ship were satisfactory.

Two-way VHF contact was next established with British weather ship *Jig*, and although passing this ship at 140 miles range and therefore out of radar fixing range, VHF contact was maintained for 25 minutes, and Aldergrove landing weather was received both in TAFOT and in clear.

The latter weather forecast was useful in that it enabled a decision to be made well in advance of E.T.A. on the type of let-down to be carried out.

By the end of the second hour the aircraft was cruising at 42,000 ft at 0.805/228, using 7000/7000 rpm.

During the third hour power was increased to 7300 in order to increase cruising speed to 0.81/240 at 40,000 ft, and the aircraft was flying during this period through the tops of high cloud.

During the let-down a fixed throttle surge was experienced on both engines under conditions identical with those on the outward flight. Bush Mills was worked on the radio compass from 300–400 miles and finally the let-down was carried out with Nutts Corner beacon monitored by VHF homing bearings from Aldergrove. This combination of aids functioned sufficiently satisfactorily to allow a descent through cloud into conditions of reduced visibility in rain which involved the loss of not more than 2–3 minutes in time.

After landing at Aldergrove the aircraft was fully serviceable and was flown back to base at Warton one hour later.

Take-off Gander:	13.10 B.S.T.
Landing Aldergrove:	16.39 B.S.T.
Observed time point to point:	3 hours 26 minutes
Distance:	1818 nautical miles

Recommendations

1. Cockpit heating will require improvement to cover adequately the night flying case.

2. The Loran installation would require further development to be effective.

3. The Smith's Mk.9 auto-pilot did not prove sufficiently reliable during tests to warrant its use operationally, and this installation will require further development.

4. It would be helpful if, for these special flights, the ocean weather stations could transmit weather information, and if available radar fixes, at intervals irrespective of whether or not they receive acknowledgement from the aircraft.

During the last hour the plots had confirmed ground speeds up to 630 mph, and indicated a fifteen minute saving on the ETA. The fuel margin was very comfortable and so the decision was made to go for the 'fast descent' from 150 nautical miles out.

Peter Hillwood (in the pilot's seat for this leg with the writer sampling the dubious privilege of the jump-seat) entered thick cloud at 30,000 ft which became darker and

The Canberra Mk V prepared for the 1952 Farnborough Show, soon after the double Atlantic flight.
(British Aerospace)

more turbulent as height was lost, but he persisted in holding the 500 KIAS limit impressively right down to cloud-break at 2700 ft over Lough Neagh in low visibility and rain; this was all made possible by good signals from Nutts Corner NDB monitored with VHF bearings from Aldergrove, resulting in Warton having to give only a small number of course corrections of five degrees or less, thereby simplifying the pilot's IF task.

VX185 swished across the timing point at 100 ft in the rain, with over twenty minutes in hand from the flight plan estimate; it touched down on the glistening runway ten hours and four minutes after leaving it that morning and taxied in towards the large crowd of RAF personnel, milling media-men and photographers who were clearly all rather damp.

An intentionally short Press briefing — they all had thier stories, and we had a further trip to do — and then VX185 was airborne again for Warton, without the need for refuelling even after crossing the Atlantic at close to maximum speed all the way!

At Warton there was a small (it was, after all, after 'working hours'), slightly self-conscious group of engineers and ground staff to greet their returning, and by now famous, Canberra; and after a few words on either side we, the crew, walked across the tarmac towards the offices in the quiet of the August evening.

It had been an interesting day. This latest Canberra had given further proof of the qualities of this great design. Much valuable test information had been collected, and as what seemed to us a minor bonus, massive headline publicity had been achieved for our product and British Aviation — and also the Atlantic had for the first time been crossed twice in one day.

That seemed to be a good note on which to now go home to explain our absence to our wives.

Then someone handed me a brown envelope. I put it in my pocket and opened it a few minutes later — it was a telegram from Her Majesty the Queen.

Chapter Four
Testing the First British Supersonic Fighters 1954-1958

In 1947 the British Government, on advice from the Chief Scientist, cancelled the Miles M.52 and with it Britain's very real chance of becoming the first nation to achieve full supersonic flight.

The prototype was in advanced build when a policy statement was issued saying that supersonic flight would be too dangerous and that this research could be done better and more cheaply by the RAE (Royal Aircraft Establishment) using models. This was a misjudgement of monumental proportions doomed to rapid failure, and it put Britain six years behind America in the race to achieve practical supersonic level flight and to acquire the technology necessary for the inevitable requirement for military supersonic aircraft.

The Bell XS1, the world's first supersonic aircraft. *(John W. R. Taylor)*

The Hawker P1052 on test from Langley in 1948, flown by 'Wimpey Wade.' Note the unswept tailplane.
(Flight International)

By 1953, practical research flying in the USA was well advanced in the field of supersonics, the Bell XS-1 and Douglas Skyrocket having both exceeded Mach 2 and the P-86 Sabre swept-wing fighter, with a Mach 1 dive capability, was already in service with the USAF. The North American F-100 Super Sabre was also due to fly, giving America its first operational fighter with a level flight supersonic capability.

In the late 1940s, development of the Hawker P.1052 and P.1081 research fighters had ended with the death of 'Wimpey' Wade in the P.1081. This was not allowed to deflect the main thrust towards a practical transonic fighter, but it was not until June 1951 that the Hawker P.1067 prototype, later to be named Hunter, was ready for flight.

At Supermarine, work had begun in 1948 on the development of their unsuccessful Attacker and Type 510 series, incorporating forty-degree swept wings and tailplanes; the 510 was first flown by Mike Lithgow on 29 December, but it soon showed a disappointing Mach performance due to its relatively thick wings and high drag fuselage-side engine intakes. Further development came with the Type 541 which had aerodynamic improvements and the more powerful Avon RA7 engine; but this aircraft was heavily damaged in a crash-landing in 1951 and cancelled.

Both these developments led to the Supermarine Swift fighter prototype with further improvements including an 'all-flying' tailplane to provide improved control in transonic dive recovery, as in the P-86 Sabre. The Swift also encountered many development problems, and although the first F.1 production aircraft flew soon after the prototype in 1952, it was not until February 1953 that Dave Morgan was able to dive it to Mach 1.

The Swift programme struggled on with a mounting list of aerodynamic and engineering problems, and despite dedicated efforts by Supermarine engineers, and the company test pilots led by Mike Lithgow, the Swift programme was cancelled by the RAF in February 1955 leaving the British fighter field open to Hawker with their just-into-service transonic Hunter, and to English Electric with their P.1/P.1B programme which, already well into its supersonic testing, was the sole British supersonic fighter design in sight.

The Vickers Supermarine Type 510, forerunner of the Swift series. *(John W. R. Taylor)*

An early Hawker Hunter being flown by Neville Duke from Dunsfold in 1953.

The Hunter had begun its test flying in July 1951 in the hands of Neville Duke, who dived it to Mach 1 for the first time in January 1952. It was soon shown to be a fine, managable fighter with an ability to dive to beyond the speed of sound with safe, though at this condition heavy and sluggish, control — the first British aircraft to have this capability.

It was, in fact, a P.86-class fighter, but it did not reach RAF service until 1954, six years after the XP.86's first Mach 1 flight. Those six years, from 1948 to 1954, marked precisely the period of lost competitiveness in the field of supersonics enforced on British industry and the Royal Air Force by the Government decision of 1947 — a decision which also resulted in the need to procure American P-86s for the RAF's NATO front line commitment in the early 1950'!

It was also a period in which the dedicated, and often dangerous, flying undertaken by manufacturers' test pilots was misunderstood by the public, resulting from Press, TV and Radio misinterpretation. When the Swift and Hunter displayed their sonic boom capability at the Farnborough Air Show in 1953, the Media, with their traditional and unbridled enthusiasm, declared 'the Supersonic Era has arrived!' (They had apparently overlooked the fact that it had arrived in America some six years earlier!) However, much euphoria and wildly inaccurate reporting followed, banner headlines attributing almost any 'CRASH!' to 'the Sound Barrier'.

Reality, if not normality, was to return in 1954 with the successful advent of the English Electric P.1 and the Fairey Delta — the first truly capable supersonic British aircraft. But for many years the British media continued to insist that the only way to recover from a supersonic dive was for the pilot to push the stick forward and 'reverse the controls'! — a procedure suggested by no less an authority than the film 'Sound Barrier'!

The English Electric P.1 programme had begun in 1949 with the acceptance of Teddy Petter's design proposal of the previous year, followed by the issue of a contract under Specification F23/49 for two flying prototypes and one structural test aircraft, and construction was well advanced by the end of 1953. Powered by two, off-the-shelf, Armstrong Siddeley, axial-flow Sapphire engines, each giving 7200 lb static thrust at sea level (without the reheat thrust augmentation which was to come later), the P.1 prototypes were designated as 'research aircraft with fighter strength factors' which could be developed straightforwardly into operational fighters if successful; they were in fact technology demonstrators.

Having arrived at Boscombe Down in the spring of 1954 (to take advantage of its 3000 yd runway), WG 760 was taxied for the first time on 22 July 1954. On 24 July the author carried out a lift-off and straight hop of about 500 yd at 125-140 kts before landing smoothly and comfortably on Boscombe's long, gently undulating, main runway.

The roll-out of Britain's first truly supersonic aircraft: the English Electric P1, serial WG760, at Boscombe Down, July 1954. *(British Aerospace)*

WG760 on preparation for its first flight, 4 August 1954. *(British Aerospace)*

Everything was encouraging and on 4 August, the P.1, Britain's first fully supersonic aircraft, was ready for its first flight:

English Electric Co Ltd
F23/49 WG760 Flight Report No. 1
Weather conditions
Dry runway; light variable wind at ninety-degrees to the runway, backing; six-eighths high cloud; small amount scattered low cloud; visibility four-to-five miles in slight haze. Runway 24.

A full cockpit check was carried out which revealed no defective items except for the leg straps on the Mk 3 ejection seat. The individual leg harnesses had been checked previously but the lacing had not been completed during those checks. On coupling the lacing in accordance with the maker's instructions, it was found that the lacings were required to inter-connect between the left and right leg. With feet on the rudder pedals this resulted immediately in a severe restriction of backward control movement. After re-checking, it was decided that flight could be accepted without the leg harnesses owing to the existing speed limitation and the circumstances of the flight.

Radio checks with the Tower and Flight Test van were satisfactory. Stopwatch failure soon after initial tripping prevented a time record being taken of the flight. Instrumentation was switched on after start-up.

Take-off was made with flaps down and without attempting to lift off at the lowest possible speed. After lifting the nosewheel, at approximately 120 kt, the aircraft became airborne easily with slightly under full elevator at approximately 145 kt. The attitude was checked immediately on becoming airborne with a small amount of forward stick, and as the aircraft gained speed it became progressively nose-up out-of-trim.

The undercarriage was selected 'up' at approximately 160 kt and power was reduced to maintain approximately 200 kt in a shallow climb. The undercarriage retracted rapidly with slight asymmetry which caused a small lateral displacement. This was over-corrected with aileron control which, under these conditions, was very sensitive but the resultant oscillation was damped immediately by centring and momentarily relaxing stick hold. The undercarriage locked home before 200 kt, and as speed was gradually increased above this point buffet was noticeable from the flaps.

As IAS exceeded 250 kt, the flap blow-back valve operated and the flaps returned to neutral with the selector down. This resulted in further nose-up out-of-trim, and full nose-down trim on the indicator was not sufficient to return to in-trim flight.

Speed was reduced to 200 kt, the flap selector moved to 'up' and then at 190 kt selected to 'down'. Flap operation was normal and it was noted that there was little buffet from flaps below 200 ft. Flaps were retracted at 210 kt. At this speed nose-flap only was selected and, apart from a very slight nose-down trim change, no other effects were noted (lessening of the existing nose-up condition).

The P1 shows precision controllability during its first air-photo session while being flown by the author from Boscombe Down in 1954. *(British Aerospace)*

With flaps retracted, power was increased and altitude increased to 8000–9000 ft. IAS was increased progressively up to 400 kt and at this point there was no buffeting or roughness. The ailerons, which were noticeably sensitive, became progressively more so with increase in IAS, with the result that lateral damping seemed to be rather lower than desirable. Releasing the stick in all cases damped out the lateral oscillation immediately however, and it was thought that much of this over-sensitivity in lateral control resulted from the fact that the pilot had at all times to hold a small, but noticeable, nose-up out-of-trim force.

Height was increased to 13,000–14,000 ft and speed increased to 400 kt IAS/Mach 0.75. Under these conditions the lateral control remained very sensitive but adequate. During a course alteration to avoid a cloud layer, the nose was depressed slightly and speed inadvertently increased at idling power to approximately 400–450 kt. This was reduced as soon as level flight could be resumed.

Dive brakes were checked at 300–400 kt at 13,000 ft over approximately two-to-four inches of movement. In each case, after the initial slight nose-up trim change, very heavy buffet began. This was associated with an erratic directional characteristic which immediately resulted in an erratic rolling displacement due to yaw. These circumstances were not regarded as satisfactory and the tests were discontinued, subject to further progressive investigation at low speeds.

During the climb it had not been easy to control the air conditioning with the cold air unit, as with this there was a tendency either to be too hot or too cold. The cabin air ram valve was opened and found to produce a pleasantly distributed flow of cooling air. This was kept open at all times during the flight, except for a short period at 14,000 ft where it was closed to test pressurisation which was found to be satisfactory at this height.

During the descent the inner surface of the centre armoured glass panel became misted with the NESA switch at 'half'. Switching the NESA system to 'full' cleared this condition in a few minutes. With power reduced to idling, considerable difficulty was experienced in obtaining a reasonable rate of descent while keeping IAS below 400 kt. This may tend to be a minor limiting factor in flight test operation if the present dive brakes prove unsatisfactory.

With the fuel state at 1000/1000 lb it was decided to return to base, and during this some difficulty was experienced at a critical point in obtaining homing facilities from Boscombe.

Once the circuit had been regained, circuit manoeuvrability at 359–250 kt proved excellent with vision forward and sideways rather better than on the Hunter. Turns at and up to 2.5 g were comfortably executed with nose-flap 'up', and with nose-flap 'down' turns up to 2 g at 250–300 kt were again positively stable.

In a proving flight of this description a detailed appraisal of feel is not possible, but the increase in Q-feel forces on the tailplane control with increase in IAS, seemed to be precisely suitable.

The undercarriage was selected 'down' at 230 kt and locked rapidly with green indicator lights at 210 kt. There was asymmetry in this operation which resulted in the expected lateral displacement and corresponding momentary overcorrection with aileron. This case is similar to that experienced on the Hunter.

Flaps were lowered at 200 kt and in doing so returned the aircraft to in-trim longitudinally, still with full nose-down trim. A final turn was carried out at 200–190 kt, and speed reduced to 160 kt at short finals and the throttles reduced to idling. A normal hold-off was made crossing the boundary, and a final check comfortably and easily executed at 150 kt. The touchdown was smooth, at a reasonable attitude with exellent vision of the runway, at approximately 140 kt.

The parachute was streamed at approximately 135 kt, and this operated with a delay of the order of two seconds. There was an immediate nose-up pitch and weathercock yaw to starboard, requiring approximately full port rudder to hold. This condition was easily controlled, and once the nosewheel had returned to the runway light wheel brake was applied to bring the aircraft to a standstill. The parachute jettisoning operation was satisfactory. At standstill the port wheel thermo-couples indicated 160°C.

During the flight a pitot position-error check was carried out with the pacing Canberra (WH 775) and this gave 195/195 kt at 8000 ft.

Summary
1. The main services functioned satisfactorily, with the exception of the dive brakes which gave heavy buffet, even at the small angles employed.
2. The trim actuators were satisfactory on rudder and aileron, but that on the tailplane control provided inadequate nose-down trim.
3. Longitudinal and directional static stability was positive in all flight conditions experienced so far. The aircraft was neutrally stable laterally with adequate damping, stick-free.
4. Tailplane feel and response was entirely satisfactory under all conditions, and there was no sign of over-sensitivity leading to pilot-induced oscillation. Aileron response and spring feel very sensitive and powerful, and required a light touch to prevent fairly continuous over-correction. It was not easy to apply this light touch owing to the necessity of holding off nose-up out-of-trim force throughout the whole flight with engines above half power. This aileron condition may be less noticeable when the longitudinal trim range has been adjusted suitably.
5. The power control circuits were remarkably free from noticeable friction or backlash.
6. The engines were used as required and no detailed attention was paid to engine conditions beyond observing the limitations. They responded normally and entirely satisfactorily to all requirements.

In this short flight the aircraft proved to be pleasant and straightforward to fly, with the take-off and landing operations lacking in complication. The over-sensitivity in lateral control will require careful observation during subsequent tests.

Defects
Martin-Baker seat lacing restricts travel of stick.
Insufficient nose-down trim.
Check Nos. 1 and 2 radio on 122,5 and 131.3 mHz.
Air brake buffet unacceptable.

With no major problems on Flight 1, a successful Flight 2 was made on 5 August, reaching 30,000 ft and Mach 0.98 indicated, where control and stability were found to be excellent.

Correction of instrumentation results after this flight showed the actual true speed reached in level flight had been approximately Mach 1, and that a few more seconds at full power would have reached the shock-wave 'jump-up' on the pitot system and the P.1 would have been supersonic.

With only a few non-critical defects to carry forward to a suitable lay-up point for rectification, Flight 3 was set up for 11 August.

Taking the P.1 in its exhilaratingly steep climb straight to 40,000 ft (a new test point) in fine, clear weather, the author turned east over Swanage and began a level, full-throttle acceleration up the Solent towards Selsey Bill which appeared and passed underneath remarkably quickly.

With the Machmeter again apparently sticking at 0.98, the control responses in pitch, roll and yaw were judged to be in almost ideal harmony and needing only a minor gearing change to make them perfect for this condition.

There was much to observe and record at this potentially historic point — the first British aircraft at Mach 1 in level flight. But now, would it go any further?

The stopwatch showed four minutes since Mach 0.9 and suddenly, with no vibration or other warning, the Mach needle jumped from 0.98 to 1.01 — supersonic!

There was much work to be done here quickly. Engines and systems health checks, cabin conditioning, fuel state (rapidly dwindling); and then three-axis control responses checked again, and finally the vitally important directional stability Nv check by stick-free dutch roll. These all proved satisfactory, and the now low fuel state demanded reduction of power to 'idle' and a turn the quickest way round on to the heading for base.

With rapidly increasing confidence, the author swung the P.1 left over West Sussex, pulling 2 g in a thirty-degree bank on to the new heading as the Machmeter dropped back to subsonic, this time with a slight tremor and a small nose-up trim change as the shock-wave moved forward ahead of the aircraft again. Britain had a supersonic aeroplane, and one whose handling was already superb!

With Boscombe in sight ahead, a short burst of throttle in the shallow dive passing through 36,000 ft caused the Machmeter to briefly jump up again to 1.01, then the descent continued at Mach 0.9, and Boscombe Down was well aware of the P.1's sonic boom before we landed!

The trials made rapid progress and in twenty flights during the next four weeks the initial handling envelope was cleared, including supersonic to Mach 1.2, landing in moderate crosswinds and on wet runways, and also close formation for photography which at once confirmed the high quality precision of the power control system.

Some areas requiring alteration had been identified, such as slight aileron over-sensitivity at specific points in the flight envelope, and also some initially mysterious and apparently random variations in directional and lateral trim. On 26 August in a sortie devoted to this problem, the author found that these variations were related to increasing or decreasing power. For example: throttles 'forward', produced nose-up and left-wing-low trim change; and throttles 'back', the reverse!

In fact the P.1 was suffering from an unexpected effect of the high-precision, low-friction power control circuit. With very low static friction levels, slight out-of-static-balance was reacting to variations in longitudinal acceleration and causing small control inputs undemanded by the pilot! When the throttles were moved forward firmly with the stick free, the latter could be seen to move back slightly and to the left, and vice versa. The system would need full static-balancing!

The P1 on test at Warton in 1955. *(British Aerospace)*

However these, together with some systems defects, were acceptable in the short term, and on 23 September the author flew the P.1 back to Warton to commence the main and exhaustive test programme in which, over the next three years, 703 flights were made to establish the viability of its successor, the P.1B, as a practical supersonic fighter for the RAF.

The P.1B retained the basic and well proven aerodynamics and controls of the P.1, but had a virtually all-new fuselage, cockpit, and engine installation incorporating two Rolls-Royce RA24R engines, together giving approximately 30,000 lb of reheat thrust — and the first flight take-off weight was less than 30,000 lb! The prototype, XA 847, began its flight trials in April 1957, and 4 April promised to provide an exhilarating experience for the author:

English Electric Co Ltd
F23/49 XA 847 Flight Report No. 1, Warton
Pilot: R. P. Beamont
Alterations since Taxi No. 1
No. 25 two-stream brake parachute installed (Type 17 High Speed Stream). All taschengurts removed; 15 ft 9 in cable with clamps fitted; eye end with modified ferrule and side plate assembly; shroud lines from skirt to keeper 16 ft 0 in.
Checks carried out during engine runs of alternator and turbine warning light failure; found satisfactory. No action.

Preflight checks

After connecting parachute and seat harnesses, it was found that the loose adjustment portions of the lower port straps, together with buckles, overhung the canopy jettison handle and obscured vision of this. Direct access to this handle was also obstructed by these straps.

The aircraft oxygen hose was not clipped to the starboard lower seat harness. The emergency oxygen bottle had no separate manual operation, and it was apparently intended that the pilot should operate this by pulling on the cable. This did not appear to be a practical operation owing to the geometry of the cockpit and of the cable concerned, and this limited the altitude for the subsequent flight.

Engine starts and checks were satisfactory and all warning lights and indicators were 'out' with engines at thirty-one/fifty-four per cent power, j.p.t. (jet pipe temperatures) 540/480°C.

Hydraulics: 3000 lb/per square inch.

Flap operation and indication: satisfactory.

Dive brake operation and indication: satisfactory.

In taxying with engines at thirty-one/fifty-four per cent there were no further system warnings, with the exception that No. 1 oil pressure blinker showed an intermittent 'white'. This was eliminated by increasing to 35 per cent.

The prototype of the Lightning, English Electric P1B, serial XA847, at Warton prior to its first flight, May 1957. *(British Aerospace)*

The P1B on its first flight, Warton, 1957. *(British Aerospace)*

Take-off was made with engines at 100/100 per cent (cold thrust) and was smooth and straightforward, with an acceleration of a similar order to WG 760 with reheat, but without the usual high noise and vibration level associated with that aircraft's engine installation.

Undercarriage retraction was smooth and symmetrical, and the climb away was held steeply in order to maintain speed below 300 kt initially.

Power was reduced to seventy/seventy per cent at approximately 5000 ft and all systems checked before reaching 10,000 ft. No abnormalities were found and the climb was continued at mach 0.9 to 27,000 ft. At this height, at 0.8 IMN (Indicated Mach Number) power was reduced, and at seventy/seventy per cent a sharp increase in noise level occurred of a type normally associated with cabin venting, an ill-fitting canopy, or other airflow noises. It was found that this noise increase was associated with engine speed, and would come in as power was reduced to seventy per cent and stop on increase above seventy per cent, at will.

A maximum cold thrust acceleration was carried out reaching 1.13 IMN, 495 kt IAS, 25,500 ft without buffet vibration or significant trim variation and power was then reduced slightly to eighty per cent. At this point the noise increase occurred again, and deceleration from Mach 1, and the subsequent descent at Mach 0.9, was accomplished by employing half dive brake, with engines maintained at eighty per cent, in a spiral descent at 2–3 g. The increased noise level conditions did not occur below 15,000 ft, where both engines could be throttled to idling.

Dive brake checks were carried out up to 400 kt IAS and 0.9 IMN and these were found to be very effective. There was no buffet or noticeable trim change up to deflection in excess of fifty per cent, but at approximately sevety-five per cent on the gauge buffeting began which, at 400 kt, was quite severe. Associated with this buffet was a mild, erratic directional wander. At all points reduction of dive brake deflection to less than seventy-five per cent eliminated this directional characteristic and reduced the buffet to negligible proportions.

Subsequent use of the dive brakes for closing into formation with the chase aircrft demonstrated their efficiency in this role.

During descent fuel contents were checked at 1100/1100 lbs at 0+17, and an idling descent was continued into the circuit.

General control characteristics in this flight had been almost identical to those of the first and second prototypes with unmodified wings, and aileron control had the early P.1 characteristics of slight over-sensitivity at transonic speeds. Buffet thresholds under g seemed to be virtually indentical with those of the first prototypes without modified leading edge. Transition through Mach 1 occurred without buffet or vibration and with even less trim change between Machs 0.9 and 1.00 than on the previous aircraft.

The nose-up trim change characteristic during deceleration transonic under g was of the same order and occurred at approximately 0.96 IMN.

Circuit and approach characteristics were quite normal, and undercarriage lowering occurred with more symmetry and therefore less disturbance than on the previous prototypes.

The final turn was made at approximately 200 kt and characteristics on the approach were normal until, when initiating the hold-off at approximately 170 kt IAS, the rate of change in pitch from full tailplane deflection was found to be rather less than that of the P.1. This resulted in a touchdown at almost constant attitude, but without a high rate of descent.

The tail parachute was streamed satisfactorily after touchdown but required a heavy force to operate the small handle. This operation was difficult. Mild braking was used during the landing run and did not result in judder. Steering and control on the runway were excellent.

Summary
The first impressions left by this flight were or a marked reduction in engine and airflow noise level in the conditions tested, and of greatly improved comfort, convenience and vision in the cockpit.

Stability and control responses were clearly recognisable as those of the standard-wing P.1A, and transition to supersonic speed occurred with the complete lack of buffet and little trim change characteristics of that aircraft.

Mild buffet roughness was apparent at subsonic speeds under g under similar circumstances to the P.1A with standard wing.

Airbrake operation was smooth and trouble-free with excellent retardation at up to two-thirds deflection. Buffeting was present above this.

Handling was therefore straightforward with the characteristics that had been expected, but made unexpectedly pleasant by the greatly reduced noise level and engine vibration level in comparison with the first two prototypes.

Defects
None requiring action before next flight.

This trouble-free and inspirational first flight was to herald an even more rapid and successful programme of tests to clear the initial handling to the specification Mach number of 1.7 and beyond. This was completed in thirty-seven flights over the next two months with excellent results which gave confidence that, though the engineering and weapons systems trials were still in the future, the basic stability, control and performance qualities of this tremendous fighter were already established. This was confirmed by a Summary Report, written by the author and issued at Warton on 5 June 1957:

Conclusions
At this early stage, therefore, the aircraft has been cleared to design Mach Number, and has indicated clearly that the performance required for the operational case will be achieved without difficulty.

Lightning development aircraft XG308 testing the Firestreak missile installation in 1958. *(British Aerospace)*

Some minor engineering defects such as undercarriage sequencing, reheat ignition and stability, and cold air unit failure, have occurred, but no design defects have been detected in tests up to the maximum design speed which could be expected to require lengthy development work.

An excellent start has therefore been made to the work of developing this aircraft up to full operational standard, and from the stability, control and performance aspects there do not appear at present to be any further problems.

It is perhaps significant to recall that excellent standards of control and stability have been obtained at supersonic speed without the use of any form of autostability. At the maximum speed so far investigated, Mach 1.75/1161 mph(T), with obviously more to come, satisfactorily positive Nv was measured by the stick-free dutch-roll method, confirming the wind-tunnel predictions, and this gives cause for confidence in the similar calculations on the increased fin area to cover the 'Blue Jay' case.

At this stage I feel confident that the main obstacles on the airframe side have been passed, and that the way is clear for the final effort on the integrated weapons system.

The large fin development for the Lightning Mk. 3, Mk. 2A, Mk. 6 and export variants, on test in 1959. *(British Aerospace)*

Britain had not only closed the aforementioned six-year gap in its progress towards achieving supersonic flight, but, by 1958, was on an equal footing with America and France. (It was thought that Russian technology had not yet become competitive, although the MiG-15 swept-wing fighter, having a performance generally similar to the P-86 Sabre, was already in service.) The P.1B Lightning was now, in fact, seen to be directly comparable in operational terms with France's Mirage and America's F-106, but was faster in the climb and more manoeuvrable than either of them; and it completely outclassed the F-104 Starfighter.

During the next five years the remarkable qualities of the Lightning were established and to some extent developed, although not by any means to its full potential — again as a result of under-estimate and wrong decision by the government of the day.

The Mach 2.2, 70,000-plus ft Lightning remained in front line service with the RAF for twenty-seven years and throughout sustained its reputation as the finest single-seat, all-weather fighter of its time; and even in its final phase-out year, 1988, it was outdated only by the weapons systems of F-16- and F-15-class fighters, but could still match them in performance and handling.

76

Throughout a decade of continuous development testing on the Lightning, a wide range of systems and configuration changes were tested in clearing eight marks and variants into RAF service, and four more for export. In these trials the great majority were straightforward and interesting, but inevitably a few unexpected occurrences sharply concentrated the minds of all concerned.

Typical of the former was the first flight programme of the cambered-leading edge modification to the wing in conjunction with the enlarged belly fuel tank, which ultimately led to the final Mk.6 and Mk.53 development of the Lightning. This work had been carried out at the Filton factory of BAC and the first flight, though successful, had been inhibited by communications problems.

In a too-fast-to-be-legal low fly-past on a humid day, a Lightning Mk. 1 gives a classic demonstration of the transonic shock waves! *(British Aerospace)*

Lightning Mk.3 development aircraft fitted with an experimental long ventral fuel tank for evaluation of the 'Mk.6' standard, being flown by the author soon after first flight at Filton. *(British Aerospace)*

The same aircraft testing the ultimate Lightning Mk.6 configuration with ferry tanks and flight-refuelling probe.

With the aircraft, XP697 (before modification a Mk.3), fully serviceable, flight 2 included delivering the aircraft back to the main test base at Warton as described in the Flight Report:

British Aircraft Corporation (Operating) Ltd
Preston Division

Experimental Flight Report	**Lightning Mk.3 XP697**
Flight No:	4
Date:	17 April 1964
Aircraft type:	Lightning Mk.3
serial no.:	XP697
Object of test:	Handling assessment.
	Long range ventral configuration with cambered leading edge.
	Delivery, Filton to Warton.
Pilot:	R. P. Beamont

Take-off loading

Total	36,388
Fuel (galls)	
residual	506 lb
port usable	2788.5 lb
starboard usable	2788.5 lb
ventral	3000 lb
total	9073 lb
C.G. position at take-off	7.65′ aft of datum
Take-off time:	14.41 (Filton)
Landing time:	15.33 (Warton)
Total:	00.52

Engine starts:

No.1:	Max. JPT 550°C at fast idle.
No. 2:	Three 'A' failures, starting on 4th attempt with max. JPT 520°C at fast idle.
Services hydraulics:	3000 psi
Brakes hydraulics:	3100 psi
Generator:	28 volts
Standby generator:	28 volts
Compass checks:	
Main	240
E2B	238
Standby D.I.	238
Take-off:	Runway 28, wind 190°/16 kt
Fuel:	2450/2400/2700 lbs
Instrumentation:	FAST
Fuel at a radar climb point:	2250/2300/2100 lbs

Initial climb at 500 kt, and power reduced at 20,000 ft due to A.T.C.

Trims:

30,000 ft   0.9   2400/2450/1200 lbs   Rudder zero
Aileron zero
Tailplane 0.7 nose-down

Instrumentation from FAST to SLOW at top of climb.

40,000 ft   0.9   2450/2500/700 lbs

Stable cruise conditions set up on track for Warton. Accurate power settling took longer than normal with approximately ten minutes required to obtain sufficiently stable conditions for the required three minutes FAST record.

39,800 ft   0.91   2450/2500/100 lbs   89/89%

TACAN check on Burtonwood and Valley, both unserviceable, and in absence of Warton radar the sortie was continued under Ulster radar control.

Reheat relights satisfactory at 30,000 ft/0.9, 100/101%, 770/780°C, nozzles maximum/maximum.

No buffet, vibration or trim change in 1g transition. Tendency to pilot-induced oscillation in pitch (no auto-stabilisers) at M=1.1.

Trims: M=1.2/39,000 ft   Rudder 0.1 port
                                Aileron 0.1 starboard
                                Tailplane 0.8 nose-down

Instrumentation FAST   Left rudder stick-free dutch roll,
                                   M=1.25
                                Damping in 4 cycles

Transition in a 2 turn with airbrakes giving 0.3 g increment on jump-down 1.0–0.97. No buffet vibration until passing 0.96 at 26. Fuel 2300/2300/0 lbs.

In continued descent at 0.8 some moderate clear turbulence was encountered in the neighbourhood of 20,000 ft, and this resulted in slight dutch roll which persisted until passing out of the turbulent layer at 15,000 ft.

Trims at low level commencing with fuel at 2200/2500/0 lbs.

7000 ft   300   1900/2100 lbs   86/87%
7000 ft   270   1900/2000 lbs   75/75%
7000 ft   248   1850/2000 lbs
6300 ft   223   1700/1800 lbs   75/75%

Undercarriage lowering at 230 kt, 8.5 seconds. However handling in the landing configuration in moderate turbulence confirmed the impression gained on the first flight that without auto-stabilisation there is a slight but not significant deterioration in pitch and yaw damping at normal circuit speeds, and that this deterioration is of an order which can be expected to be covered adequately by auto-stabilisers.

Overshoots were carried out at progressive reductions of V_r as follows:

Overshoot 1:   Runway 26
                                Wind 360°/8 kt
                                Vappr. 180 kt
                                Fuel 1300/1400 lbs
                                Attitude nose low
                                Control response on all three
                                   axes, satisfactory

Overshoot 2:   Vappr. 170 kt
                      Fuel 1200/1250 lbs
                      Attitude normal
                      Control response on all three
                          axes, satisfactory

Overshoot 3:   Vappr. 165 kt
                      Fuel 950/1050 lbs
                      Attitude rather nose high
                      Lateral response noticeably
                          sluggish below 170 kt

Landing: Runway 26
                      Wind 360°/8 kt
                      Fuel 600/650 lbs
                      Vappr. 170 kt, flare 165 kt,
                          touchdown 151 kt. Pitch control in the flare
                          satisfactory though rather less positive than
                          in the cambered leading edge configuration
                          without long range ventral.
                      Touchdown attitude normal.
                      Tail parachute satisfactory.
                      Maximum wheel braking satisfactory.

Summary

Handling at low and high speeds without auto-stabilisers was adequate, but subject to low damping affecting control conditions adversely in subsonic cruise, in pitch damping at transonic speed, and in slight pilot-induced short period pitching oscillations in the range $M=1.05–1.15$ at 40,000 ft.

Reduced aileron response in the landing configuration at C_L equivalent to 165 kt or lower at this landing weight, resulted in the need for larger than normal lateral stick displacements in crosswind or turbulent conditions.

The long range ventral tank fuel system transfer functioned satisfactorily throughout.

In this and the first flight no adverse handling characteristics were apparent resulting from the long range ventral tank and cambered leading edge configurations which would affect safe and satisfactory operation, and the slight deteriorations in damping noted should be covered adequately by auto-stabilisation.

The significant increase in fuel load made practical by this tank installation will have immediate results in the flight development successful flying rate.

Defects

1. TACAN unserviceable. No locks.
2. Engines not on top Temperature Control at altitude.

An example of the unexpected arising occurred a year later and was rather more dramatic.

The prototype Lightning Mk.5 two-seat operational trainer had been progressively exploring the roll/inertia coupling characteristics in order to meet the requirements for Service Release; and these tests had involved rolling under G in progressively more severe conditions and higher Mach numbers, when on flight no. 263 it all became rather more dramatic, as very experienced Lightning experimental test pilot J. L. (Jimmy) Dell reported:

Accident to Prototype Lightning Mk.5
Lightning Mk.5
Prototype   XM966
Flight No: 263
Date: 12 July 1965
Crew
   Pilot: J. Dell
   Flight Test Observer: G. Elkington
Object of Test: Supersonic Rapid Rolling with
                                      2 inch Rocket Pack extended
Flight conditions: Mach 1.8/650 kt/35,000 ft/3g
Weather: Minus 72°C at 35,000 ft, no cloud,
                                      good visibility
Controlling agent: Killard Point Radar

Following the loss of Lightning Trainer prototype XM966, development was continued using XM967, flown here by Jimmy Dell over the Pennines. *(British Aerospace)*

Good level acceleration achieved due to the extremely low temperature, reaching Mach 1.82/660 kt/35,000 ft before rolling into a 3g turn to port, extending the rocket pack and switching instrumentation on. Full right stick was then applied whilst still holding 3g. Aircraft initially rolled smoothly then roll rate reduced as expected, due to side-slip.

As a wings level, nose-high attitude was reached the roll-rate reduced to zero, a loud crack was heard and the aircraft departed violently to the left — obviously some serious failure had occurred.

Next recollection was of a bang and a strong draught — this was the canopy and Elkington's seat departing — and of the aircraft being inverted at a shallow nose-down angle. I was conscious of swinging like a pendulum and seeing the outside of the windscreen (head level with the windscreen arch) and the sea. (The instrumentation pack was subsequently recovered from the sea bed and analysis showed that we had been subjected to high 'g' forces and had obviously 'blacked out' during the rapid deceleration of the aircraft and although Elkington had ejected at 35,000 ft the aircraft had slowed down considerably).

Aircraft appeared to swing through 180/360° in a lateral sense before reversing and from my inverted position I could see North Wales, Isle of Man, Lake District and Southern Scotland as the aircraft oscillated. Heard very faintly Killard Point Radar calling 'Tarnish Six' (my call-sign). I had difficulty reaching up into the cockpit to operate the radio 'press to transmit' button on the throttle. Finally, managed with difficulty and transmitted 'Tarnish Six, May-day, May-day, May-day'. I then made efforts to leave the aircraft. I realised that although the seat straps, including the recently introduced Y-strap for negative G-restraint, had been specially tightened at the beginning of the flight, they had somehow loosened, hence the pendulum effect and the fact that I could not reach the ejection seat face blind as it was below shoulder level, also realised that not being in contact with the seat, if I did manage to eject I would inevitably suffer back damage. Nevertheless, I only briefly considered undoing the seat harness for a free drop.

After repeated efforts and a fleeting thought that Marjorie, my wife, would not be too pleased when she hears of this, I finally managed to reach the seat pan ejection handle and initiated the ejection. Following a sharp kick-in-the-pants and some slight tumbling the automatics operated, the seat and main parachute opened with a reassuring crack. As the seat was fitted with a 10,000 ft barostat for automatic seat operation I realised I was at or below this altitude. After a short period of stabilisation I was in a steady descent — it was a nice sunny day with no cloud, and the sea looked calm. I watched the aircraft falling below me, still inverted and oscillating until it hit the sea and vanished very quickly.

I had a strange detached feeling and remember thinking that having managed to eject I would now possibly drown in the Irish Sea, but was not unduly perturbed at the thought. Assuming that Elkington had ejected at high altitude, high speed in an extremely cold environment (−72°C) I reckoned his chances of survival were nil. However, something made me look up and I was mildly surprised to see Elkington's parachute about 300 ft above me and 300 yards to one side. He hung limply in his harness as indeed I did.

I had to force myself to take an interest in the proceedings and took off my flying helmet to drop as I approached the sea as an aid in judging my height. Unfortunately, having dropped the helmet we both hit the sea at the same time. As I came to the surface I inflated the Mae West but became entangled in the parachute rigging lines and efforts to disentangle were to no avail and increased my feeling of extreme weariness. My next action was to inflate the dinghy and I managed to crawl aboard with some difficulty still festooned with the rigging lines. After a short rest I removed the Sarbe Beacon from my Mae West, rigged the aerial on the dinghy and switched it on. I then attempted to cut through the parachute rigging lines with my aircrew knife. This was a tedious business with little success and when I eventually dropped the knife in the bottom of the dinghy I lost interest in that activity. I had to keep fighting off the detached 'it's not happening to me' feeling. And then remember looking at my watch and thinking if I'm picked up within an hour Marjorie and I might make it to the Headquarters Fighter Command Summer Ball (we had an invitation for that evening and had planned to attend). At one stage I looked around and saw Elkington's dinghy with him in it about 300 yards away so he was obviously still alive. About this time a Canberra and a Shackleton aircraft circled around us and I made a feeble attempt to wave. Sometime after, I heard the sound of the search and rescue helicopter from behind me but didn't have the energy to turn around to look. I also became aware of an intermittent bubbling sound and realised that the dinghy was deflating. It was later established, that when I dropped the aircrew knife it punctured the dinghy. The bubbling sound was the air escaping through the water sloshing around the floor of the dinghy.

The downwash from the Chopper followed by the appearance of the Winchman restimulated my thoughts of the Summer Ball. I warned the Winchman that I had hurt my back and I think he did his best but his 'bear hug retrieval' was felt, although the most uncomfortable period was lying flat on the bare metal floor of the Chopper cabin whilst picking up Elkington and during transit to the hospital at Whitehaven. On initial examination we were found to be suffering from hypothermia which had to be countered before further examination and treatment.

The rescue operation was well co-ordinated and the time of one hour from May-day call to pick-up was extremely good considering that the helicopter was based at RAF Valley in Anglesey and the pick-up approximately 76 N. Miles North North East. The rescue was triggered by the alert radar controller at Killard Point who noticed an overlaying of aircraft paints of successive radar sweeps when there should have been a considerable gap — made a radio check and then received my May-day call.

The feeling of detachment and remoteness is probably the brain's cushioning barrier in times of extreme stress on shock, and had been experienced by myself on a previous occasion.

Fortunately, both crew members made good recoveries and soon returned from hospital to flying duties, as had J. W. C. Squire (Johnny) after a similar accident to the first mark (T4) Lightning Trainer some years earlier.

These failures resulted from yawing instability causing structural failure of the fin, and were typical examples of the high risks encountered during the evolution of safe supersonic flight.

Chapter Five
Testing Second Generation American Jet Fighters, 1958

In the spring of 1958, following four years of successful research and development flying on the English Electric P.1 (first flight August 1954) and P.1B (Lightning) prototypes, it had become apparent that the breakthrough to a new threshold — practical flight at twice the speed of sound — was already in sight.

In Britain the P.1B was test-flying well at Mach 1.8, with more to come; as was the Mirage prototype in France, and a number of new American fighter prototypes were approaching Mach 1.5. Meanwhile in California the X-series of rocket-powered, experimental aeroplanes had pioneered Mach 2 and beyond; and now a new military prototype, the Lockheed XF-104, was well into its test programme and had reached Mach 2.

This was an appropriate time to gain further experience and, accordingly, the Ministry of Supply arranged a visit by the author to evaluate some of the 'Century'-series fighters, in exchange for a similar opportunity in the future for the USAF to assess the Lightning.

Following an initial briefing on the test status and future roles of the F-102 series, the F-104 and the F-106, by the respective project test pilots at the USAF test centre, Edwards AFB, (together with Captain Robert Rushworth — later an X-15 astronaut

A General Dynamics (Convair) F102 all-weather day and night fighter over California in 1958. *(General Dynamics)*

— who was appointed to be my escorting officer and who would also fly 'chase' in an F-100 on all my subsequent flights), the first flight of the series took place at nearby Palmdale, at the great Convair (later General Dynamics) production and test facility.

After a thorough professional briefing followed by a familiarization flight in a side-by-side two-seat TF-102 with USAF test pilot Capt Torres on 23 June, two flights were carried out in new-production F-102s. This was the final flight test report:

F-102
Flight Report No. 3

Aircraft:	F-102A No. 7866
Engine:	J57/P23
Date:	25 June 1958, Convair Production, Palmdale, California
Fuel:	7050 lb
Weight:	28,000 lb
Limitations:	Mach 1.5/655 kt
Flight time:	50 min

After the previous flight, attention was given to seat adjustment and it was confirmed that, at the full sitting height which was easily achieved with use of the electrically-operated mechanism, I was not sitting high enough to obtain the best possible view forward over the nose for take-off and climb.

After engine start the radar was set up and definition was excellent at maximum brilliance. Shrouding of the scope is by a supported heavy rubber moulding which is well finished and efficient. The scope is in a perfect position for scanning between external vision and instrument reference, but the arrangement is spoilt by the presence of the visual gunsight, suspended from the apex of the vee windscreen arch where it obstructs vision to some extent.

Engine starts and checks were satisfactory.

Taxying again noticeably easier than the TF-102 (side-by-side two-seat trainer variant), owing to the nosewheel steering mechanism remaining selected after initial operation of the stick button. The gearing of the nosewheel steering was still felt to be too coarse, and some over-corrections were made.

After setting ratiometer (thrust indicator) at 2.02 and increasing power to maximum cold at ninety-three per cent thrust, 595°C, brakes were released and reheat engaged with rotation outboard of the throttle. As soon as reheat had stabilised the throttle was increased to maximum reheat power and the nosewheel was lifted off at 125 kt, with the aircraft flying off smoothly at 145 kt. Reheat throttle operation was checked following the recent defect (on Flight 2) and on cutting to cold this was found to be satisfactory. Reheat was reselected at 5000 ft and a timed climb resumed as follows:

HEIGHT (AMSL)	SPEED			
10,000 ft	Mach .75/350 kt	92.5 per cent 600°C 5600 lb	Zero (stopwatch)	Max reheat
20,000 ft	Mach .82	92.5 per cent 600°C	Zero+1.30 min	Max reheat
30,000 ft	Mach .88	91 per cent 595°C	Zero+3 min	Max reheat
36,000 ft	Mach .9	90.5 per cent 595°C 4400 lb	Zero+3.24 min	Reheat cut
At 36,000 ft a maximum cold stabilisation was checked (altimeter 29.8 millibars)				
36,000 ft	Mach .93/312 kt	Fuel: 4200 lb	Zero+3.24 min (3 min stabilisation)	

The first attempt to light reheat at this height failed, but the second was satisfactory with maximum power achieved at 90.4 per cent, 595°C, at Mach 0.93 indicated; and a maximum power acceleration was checked:

HEIGHT (AMSL)	SPEED				
36,000 ft	Mach .93t	90.4 per cent 595°C 4100 lb	Zero		Max reheat
37,000 ft	Mach 1.04/360 kt	90.4 per cent 595°C	Zero+56 sec		Max reheat
37,000 ft	Mach 1.1/372 kt	90.4 per cent 600°C 3200 lb	Zero+3 min		Max reheat
Possible small acceleration remaining					

Still with maximum reheat, a climbing turn was initiated at 0.4 g and the system jump-down occurred at 38,000 ft. Thereafter at this normal acceleration, Mach 0.95 indicated was maintained to 42,000 ft, where g was increased to 1.8 and maintained through ninety degrees of level turn. (Fuel: 3000 lb)

Control and stability with pitch and yaw dampers 'IN', but no trim servo, were satisfactory, but directional and lateral damping, following rolling displacement, were not immediately dead-beat, with noticeable adverse yaw.

Maintaining maximum reheat power, a dive was initiated, reaching Mach 1.2/ 400 kt at approximately 37,000 ft, with a dive angle of thirty to thirty-five degrees. Reheat was cut at this point (six minutes after relighting at 36,000 ft), and the fuel total checked at Mach 1 in a shallow descent in maximum cold was 2950 lb with 1200–1300 lb per side.

Before leaving 30,000 ft, a check was made of radar scope conditions, and the presentation was exceptionally clear and well-defined; as no target presented itself at this time, no further investigation could be made.

The lengthy Palmdale recovery pattern was entered with 2180 lb of fuel, and during this phase it was possible to simulate instrument recovery conditions. The stability and control response characteristics of the aircraft, with pitch and yaw dampers 'IN', resulted in an aircraft which should present no problems in instrument conditions. Control forces both in pitch and roll were felt to be on the high side, but not to a critical extent.

Manoeuvrability in the landing configuration and at circuit speeds was good, and the aircraft was well clear of its buffet boundary when pulling up to 1.5 g at 200 kt onto the final turn.

The approach was perfectly simple to carry out at the recommended speeds, and the hold-off and touchdown on the aiming point could be made repeatedly and with accuracy. The lack of landing flap felt strange on each occasion that this aircraft was flown; but it was missed only as part of the normal sequence of cockpit operation, the attitude in the approach configuration being quite normal and unexaggerated without the deployment of flaps.

This flight confirmed the following impressions:

The cockpit is spacious and reasonably well laid out, but the emergency drills are more complicated than in the majority of single-engined fighter aircraft, and require some time and attention from the pilot who is unfamiliar with the aircraft. In this connection a more concise 'flip-over'-type cockpit check-list would have been appreciated.

The view from the cockpit is seriously restricted by the vee windscreen and dividing reflection screen, the windscreen arch structure and the visual gunsight mounted at its peak, and by the metal structure of the canopy frame. This obstruction to vision is most apparent under circuit conditions when a 100 per cent visual safety search for other aircraft is impossible in the landing pattern, and also at high altitude in high-speed flight when there are significant areas forward of and above the aircraft's flight path in which the pilot cannot obtain a safe, visual scan.

With auto-stability the standards of damping and control response were high, and the aircraft should be a satisfactory instrument and weapons platform. Auto-stability made it, at all times, a pleasant aircraft to fly, but damping with yaw and pitch dampers 'OUT' was very poor on all axes above Mach 0.8 indicated, and in those conditions stability and control could be regarded only as adequate for recovery under reasonably favourable conditions. The performance is supersonic in only a narrow height band; 'operational' performance is therefore, generally speaking subsonic, but altitude performance is probably satisfactory up to more than 50,000 ft at subsonic speed.

Convair TF-102 and F-102A
Conclusions
Both the trainer and fighter versions of this aircraft are in operational service with the USAF, the F-102A being the latest standard all-weather fighter.

The performance of the fighter is supersonic in only a narrow height band and, for operational purposes, it has only slightly greater performance than the Javelin in terms of speed and altitude ability. The trainer is subsonic throughout its level-flight envelope, and can achieve supersonic speed only in a dive.

A good standard of flight control has been achieved with artificial stability, and both aircraft are good instrument platforms, with all-weather clearance to local base weather minima. They are well-liked by squadron pilots, but no information was forthcoming on the reliability of the weapons systems.

The CRT presentation was exeptionally clear however, and the general impression gained was that the system is producing good results in operation.

With auto-stabilisers and trim co-ordinator 'IN', control conditions in transition and in the landing configuration were quite satisfactory, although some adverse yaw was noticeable in manoeuvre and on the approach in rough air.

With auto-stabilisers 'OUT', damping at transonic speeds on all axes was very poor, although the aircraft could in fact be flown in this condition in an emergency.

The Convair vee windscreen was felt to be a retrograde step in comparison with the conventional arrangement of flat centre panel with two quarter panels, because vision was quite seriously restricted and because, under certain circumstances, the essential anti-reflection dividing screen interfered with forward vision.

The F-102 was felt to be a straightforward and well-developed all-weather fighter which should give valuable service under extreme weather conditions.

The F-102 had been a nice enough aeroplane to fly, and seemed to have a good potential for all-weather fighting; but, for all practical purposes, its military performance was subsonic. The next aircraft on the programme, the F-104 Starfighter, promised to be far more interesting!

The Lockheed production and test facility was on the other side of Palmdale Airport and there, on 26 June 1958, a comprehensive and distinctly serious briefing began, conducted by a combined team of USAF project test pilots and Lockheed pilots and engineers. The reason for the underlying seriousness of the briefing soon became apparent when the safety and precautionary aspects were covered. The F-104 had had an unhappy reputation since it began USAF testing in the previous year, and already nineteen test pilots had been killed. The main cause, engine flame-out, had not been eradicated at this stage, and much attention was given in briefing to all possible engine-out situations. In the main, the recommendations boiled down to one: 'Eject' — but with the proviso that if the engine flamed out on the climb below 1000 ft, or on the approach below 2000 ft, the only way out would be to roll inverted before using the downward-ejecting seat!

It was confirmed that the F-104 was cleared to Mach 2 (with very careful throttle handling to avoid compressor surge flame-out) and that 'You can try it, if you wish'!

However, the enthusiasm for this small almost wingless fighter seemed at best muted, and was overshadowed by a predominance of items which were not permitted for investigation over those which were. This was all impressive, particularly the briefing on high angle-of-attack (AOA) handling and spin avoidance, given by project pilot Dave Holloman. When strapping in to fly on the following day, the flight was delayed and a column of smoke could be seen out on the desert, marking Holloman's last flight. His 104 had flamed out when approaching to land at Palmdale, and he was too low to eject.

A production F104 on test at the Lockheed base at Palmdale, California, in 1958. *(Lockheed)*

After about an hour's delay, flying was resumed and I flew three interesting sorties. Extracts from the briefing details and the final test report on the last of these sorties follow:

Lockheed F-104A

Introduction

The discussions and briefing were held on the morning of 26 June 1958 at the Lockheed production plant, Palmdale. Capts Jordan and Rushworth (USAF Fighter Test Operations, Edwards AFB); I. Pratt (Senior Production Test Pilot, Lockheed, Palmdale); Messrs Schalk and Holloman, and D. Brown (Engineering Test Pilots, Lockheed, Palmdale); and G. Guisler (Production Flight Test Engineer, Lockheed, Palmdale) comprised the briefing team.

Status: Limited squadron service, Day/fair-weather only.

Early series aircraft were fatigue-limited to 575 kt below 30,000 ft, but with the new 'steel' tail the q limit is 800 kt equivalent airspeed. Mach limits are Mach 2 or a compressor inlet temperature flight limitation of 100°C (absolute limit 120°C)

Weights

Clean configuration:	19,502 lb
Two Sidewinders:	19,936 lb
Two Sidewinders + pylon tanks:	22,986 lb
Tip and pylon tanks:	25,057 lb

The tip tanks have been cleared to Mach 2, but are excessively draggy; the pylon tanks have been cleared to Mach 1.7, again with very heavy drag. The pylon tanks are intended purely for subsonic ferry purposes.

Engine	J79-FE-3A
Static sea level thrust:	9000 lb cold
	15,000 lb with reheat

The J79-7, which is now coming through the production line and was in one of the aircraft subsequently flown, has a 'T2 reset' modification which restricts the rate of engine deceleration in order to prevent intake buzz, and is also uprated, increasing the reheat thrust by approximately 2000 lb (sea level static).

The wingtip tanks have been jettisoned satisfactorily at Mach 1.5, and carry 165 US gallons each. The pylon tanks carry 200 US gallons each. The wingtip-mounted Sidewinders, which are standard armament in Air Defence Command, cause no flight limitations. No increase in drag has been measurable, but the small increase in aspect ratio from the tip attachment is claimed to have improved altitude handling.

A spinning programme has been completed to USAF requirements by Lockheed, and these were described by the Project Pilot, D. Holloman. The aircraft does not spin easily, as it normally enters from the stall into its characteristic pitch-up manoeuvre from which there is no recovery by direct pilot action.

Pitch-up occurs at twenty-three degrees angle-of-attack, and the aircraft then goes through a pitching and rolling manoeuvre from which recovery normally occurs, without pilot action, in the inverted position, after a height loss of 11,000–13,000 ft. In order to avoid entering this condition a vane-operated stick-shaker is fitted which operates at seventeen degrees angle-of-attack, and if, despite the stick shaker warning, the aircraft is still allowed to reach twenty degrees angle-of-attack, an auto pitch control imparts a sharp forward motion to the stick, moving the tailplane through one inch. This is effective in preventing pitch-up with all but the most determined pilots.

Spinning has had to be achieved by pro-spin control movement immediately before pitch-up, and recovery from the spin is with forward stick only, ailerons and rudder neutral. Anti-spin rudder and pros-spin aileron have prevented spin recovery. Even with the forward stick technique recovery is critical as, unless a lengthy dive-out is held, the aircraft will go into a pitch-up condition immediately on leaving the spin.

These trials have been conducted to an 'acceptable' clearance condition by the company, with observation in the air and on the ground by USAF observers. The USAF 'does not require to repeat the trials'.

Damping rates at Vmax were described, with stabilisers 'IN', as:

Yaw: deadbeat in one cycle/two sec
Roll: deadbeat in three cycles/four sec

With yaw and roll dampers 'OUT' a continuous dutch roll was present at one cycle per second, of unspecified amplitude and undamped, at all speeds supersonic and, to a lesser extent, subsonic. Directional stability (Nv) at Mach 2 was described as 'positive'. Pitch damping with stabiliser 'OUT' at Mach 2 was quoted as half amplitude in two cycles, and deadbeat in six cycles; stabiliser 'IN', one cycle/two-and-a-half-seconds to deadbeat.

In answer to a question on control effectiveness in the recent energy climbs to very high altitude, it was stated that there was adequate though sluggish aileron response, and similar control in pitch in the nose-down mode up to the maximum height reached (at that time) of 90,000 ft. At this height there was little nose-up control, owing to stabiliser trim running out.

At 90,000 ft the cabin altimeter had indicated 55,000 ft and the pilot's personal clothing (PP suit and K1/2 helmet) had pressurised automatically. (This helmet was regarded as reasonably satisfactory for experimental purposes because the flights were of short duration, and because the uncomfortable faceplate could be removed during the latter part of the descent for return to circuit and landing.

The flap-blowing system was regarded as critical in the approach configuration, and on lowering full flap the pilot was required to check for asymmetry in the flap-blowing circuit. If more than half an inch of stick displacement was required to correct in the lateral sense, the flap-blowing had to be regarded as suspect, flaps retracted, and the landing carried out with hold-off 190 kt. Wheel rotation limit 225 kt, drag chute shear link 225 kt.

Airbrakes were cleared for operation at any speed.

Considerable attention was given to engine handling, and the critical nature of the flame-out recovery was stressed in detail.

Reheat lighting was reliable below 35,000 ft, and lighting and cutting below this height were not critical. Above 35,000 ft there is a progressive uncertainty, and above 45,000 ft instability and reheat flame-out were likely in 'intermediate' and possible at any stage. Reheat flame-out would often then result in engine flame-out, and engine relighting in flight could not be relied on. Variation of reheat thrust was without rpm variation, but care had to be taken when cutting reheat to prevent reducing power below maximum cold, as this, in the unmodified engine, was liable to cause intake buzz, compressor stall and flame-out. On the 'DASH 7' engine a 'T2 reset' modification had been incorporated which restricted the rate and conditions under which cold rpm could be reduced. This did not preclude the probability of engine flame-out in the event of reheat instability and flame-out.

In view of the record of this aircraft in terms of the proportion of fatal accidents in attempted flame-out landings, it was advised that the aircraft should be abandoned in the event of not being unable to relight a flamed-out engine by

20,000 ft; after some five hours' experience on the type it was recommended that an attempt should be made to land a flamed-out aircraft on the 7-mile runway at Edwards; but this could only be done if the aircraft was positioned at a minimum of 17,000 ft over Edwards, outbound. From this point, at 240 kt IAS, a 360-degree gliding turn was made, on completion of which the pitot probe would be pointing at the point of contact with the ground. If this did not coincide with the landing end of the dry lake the pilot would abandon the aircraft. Alternatively, if the touchdown could be made on the lake, the dive/glide would be continued until passing through 2000 ft where the undercarriage would be lowered without checking glide angle, and it should then lock down when rotating for touchdown at around 200 kt/200 ft.

Some successful flame-out landings had been made in this manner, and a new one was in fact made during the first day of this visit by a Lockheed test pilot from Palmdale who landed successfully with a full compressor stall at Edwards.

Unfortunately, a large number of fatal accidents had occurred in similar circumstances and on the second day at Lockheed, Mr Holloman, the Engineering Test Pilot who had described the spinning trials, was killed just short of the runway threshold at Palmdale when an engine flamed out, apparently during a normal approach.

Vmax was limited by a compressor inlet temperature flight limit of 100°C (actual 120°C), or by Mach 2, whichever was the lower.

The cabin pressure differential was five pounds per square inch.

The downwards ejection seat system seemed unlikely, in the extreme, to provide a safe escape facility below approximately 1000 ft, and only then if the aircraft was rolled inverted before ejection.

I reported on my fourth F-104 sortie as follows:

Lockheed F-104A
Flight Report No. 6
Lockheed Production, Palmdale

Aircraft:	F-104A No. 762
Engine:	J79-7
Date:	27 June 1958
Weight:	18,886 lb
Fuel (usable):	5889 lb
Limitations:	Mach 2 or CIT 100°C 575 kt EAS below 30,000 ft
Flight time:	35 mins

After a third -104 sortie had been aborted on the runway, owing to UHF radio failure, a final sortie was successful.

As before, entry into the cockpit, seat adjustment, accessibility readability and layout of all controls and instruments were appreciated.

Engine start satisfactory, and systems and warnings normal. Engine idling sixty-eight per cent, 420°C, nozzle three-quarters.

The view on taxiing was again noticeably improved over the Convair fighters, but holding in of the nosewheel steering button on the stick was inconvenient, especially on the long taxiing involved between the Lockheed plant and the threshold of the runway in use (25, approximately 1.5 miles from start-up point). Fuel 5400 lb.

With power at ninety-five per cent, 590°C, reheat was lit by simple rotation of the throttle outboard and, after the initial roughness had steadied, power was increased to Maximum reheat with brakes off. Acceleration was of a similar order to the English Electric P.1B at maximum cold and during initial acceleration, short periods of stick-shaker vibration occurred.

Rotation was initiated at the briefed speed of 165 kt and, as the aircraft flew off smoothly, periods of stick-shaker vibration occurred on passing through rough air. This condition continued until the angle of climb was reduced very slightly, when the climb-away was continued smoothly during undercarriage retraction and landing flap retraction at 260 kt IAS.

While initiating a required traffic pattern turn to starboard at this speed the stick-shaker was again in evidence, but at upwards of 300 kt IAS normal course-changing manoeuvres could be executed without coming on to this condition. (Altimeter setting 29.9 millibars.)

HEIGHT (AMSL)	SPEED	TIME	REMARKS
16,000 ft	Mach .85	Zero+2 min	—
	Maximum reheat climb continued		
36,000 ft	Mach .88	Zero+3 min	

A 1.5 g turn to port was indicated at maximum reheat, ninety-one per cent/595°C, fuel 3850 lb. The ASI system jump-up occurred during this turn which was held through 210°, prior to levelling and continuing the acceleration.

HEIGHT (AMSL)	SPEED	TIME	REMARKS
36,000 ft	Mach 1.2	Zero+5.5 min	—
36,000 ft	Mach 1.5	Zero+6.5 min	Fuel 3000 lb
36,000 ft	Mach 1.8/500 kt IAS	Zero+7.1 min	Compressor inlet temp: 80°C
37,000 ft	Mach 2.0/700 kt IAS	Zero+8 min	Fuel: 2500 lb
Noise level and roughness increase from Mach 1.84. Compressor inlet temp 90°C and 'SLOW' light indicator flashing.			

From subsonic and throughout this acceleration a small amplitude 1 Hz directional oscillation had been present, and this was disturbing to the point of being nearly unacceptable for gun platform conditions. The yaw damper was disengaged before decelerating and the directional oscillation was immediately trebled in amplitude, although it did not become divergent.

Pitch damping with stabilisers 'IN' at this point was satisfactory, and the aircraft could be pulled into a turn and levelled out without over-correction in pitch or roll. Aileron response was noticeably more sluggish than at lower speeds, but was still adequate, although the lumpy breakout force was not liked.

Engine roughness at Mach 2 was considerable and, owing to the critical nature of the engine installation in these flight conditions, care was taken in following the briefing as closely as possible to avoid flame-out. Reheat was cut to maximum cold, and the resultant deceleration was sharp and associated with between one and two cycles of oscillation in pitch.

At Zero plus twelve minutes the descent was begun, with indicated fuel now at 2900 lb, ninety per cent/400°C, nozzle one-quarter, oil pressure forty-two pounds per square inch, hydraulics 3000 lb per square inch.

The next four minutes were devoted to navigation, as the high-speed run had taken the aircraft out of sight of Muroc on an easterly heading (over the sun-drenched mountains and desert of California). These flights are not conducted under radar or UHF/DF control, and during this phase the excellent layout of the cockpit, coupled with its simplicity and the good forward and sideways view, was again noted.

At zero plus eighteen minutes descent continued through 10,000 ft, 300 kt/ eighty-eight per cent, fuel 2250 lb; entering recovery pattern from Mojave to Rosamond Lake.

At Zero plus twenty-five minutes and 5,000 ft, rolls to right and left were carried out at 550 kt in mild turbulence, and although the ailerons were responsive and powerful, the lumpy breakout force resulted in over-correction and a tendency to become slightly out-of-phase with the high rates developed.

On rejoining the circuit with 1900 lb fuel, airframe buffet was experienced when reducing below 240 kt in the clean configuration. This was eliminated by use of landing flap, but after lowering the undercarriage, with speed steady at 220 kt downwind, the stick-shaker continued to make itself felt during passage through rough air. On pulling the turn from base leg to finals at 190 kt, the stick-shaker came in at approximately 1.3 g and continued as the turn was completed.

Directional control in turbulence during final approach was quite satisfactory, with an occasional tendency to lurch sideways. Provided that the correct approach speed of 180 kt was maintained at eighty-eight per cent, no difficulty was experienced in maintaining the approach to the correct hold-off point, although the aircraft felt critical at all times and aileron lumpiness was again disliked when correcting for rolling moment due to yaw in turbulence.

The hold-off and touchdown were straightforward provided that power was not altered from the set eighty-eight per cent, as to do this would reduce flap-blowing and cause a high rate of descent. The soft Dowty liquid-spring system undercarriage eliminated all landing shock and ensured a smooth touchdown.

After lowering the nosewheel the tail parachute handle was operated, but the parachute was not felt and it was reported by the tower that it had developed and self-jettisoned. Use of the pedal-operated wheelbrakes was smooth and decelerated the aeroplane reasonably rapidly with moderately heavy use, down to normal taxying speed in well under 2000 yd. It was again pleasant to be able to lift the sideways-opening canopy for taxying in under the hot desert sun.

The F-104 had proved to be technically fascinating, exhilarating in performance but otherwise rather unpleasant to fly and given the under-developed engine circumstances, undoubtedly rather dangerous; and the claims that it was to be a 'next generation air superiority fighter' were judged to be more than a little controversial.

The next aircraft for elvaluation, the XF-106, was still at the experimental stage and seemed likely to be much more promising than the F-104.

The briefing was held on 30 June 1958 at the Convair experimental base, Edwards AFB. The briefing team was headed by Dick Johnson (famous test pilot of Convair's delta series of aircraft, and one of America's all-time greats in test flying), and comprised company flight test specialists, the chief flight test engineer, and Capt Rushworth who was to fly chase again.

I was quickly made to feel part of the XF-106 programme, and I looked forward to trying this second-generation, supersonic, delta-winged fighter from such an experienced organisation. The reality was not disappointing.

The briefing was completed comfortably in the morning, followed by a relaxed lunch in a nearby desert diner, when almost everything else but the XF-106 was talked about. Eventually I taxied out in the second prototype (serial 6453), onto the dazzling white glare of the salt-lake air base. The aircraft seemed to be America's nearest approach to the Lightning, and the flight was going to prove interesting.

A General Dynamics XF106 over the Mojave desert, California, in 1958. *(General Dynamics)*

The briefing notes and test report follow:

Convair XF-106A
Briefing at Edwards AFB — 30 June 1958
Introduction

Mr R. L. Johnson	Convair Experimental, Edwards AFB
Colonel Lane, USAF	Edwards AFB
Captain Rushworth, USAF	Fighter Test Operations
Status:	Research and development only.
	No production standard as yet.
All-up weight:	32,540 lb
Engine:	J57-9 reheat sea-level static
	thrust (design) = 23,000 lb
Present limitations:	Mach 1.7/750 kt IAS

The Mach limitation is an engine installation limit and results from compressor stall experience from Mach 1.74 up. Since the earliest days with this aircraft (first flight December 1956) trouble has been experienced with the engine installation/duct configuration. Originally, compressor stalling was experienced in the neighbourhood of Mach 1.5, and major modifications involving variable duct geometry with an adjustable ramp and associated boundary layer bleed, raised this restriction to only Mach 1.7, and this is still regarded as a major problem. It was not possible to obtain details of the next stage in these developments. Associated with this duct problem is a performance shortfall which, at one time, was attributed to wing drag characteristics. With the Series 20 wing they are certain that the wing problem is eliminated, and that the lost performance is a question of engine installation. No details were forthcoming on the proportional loss of performance measured, but in response to a direct question it was stated that the 2 g supersonic ceiling (standard day) was now approximately 45,000 ft and this was a disappointment to them. No energy climbs have been made beyond approximately 55,000 ft, for these reasons.

95

Control and stability with pitch and yaw dampers and trim servo were described as satisfactory; as was the stall which occurs at approximately 100 kt with adequate lateral control, and longitudinal control in the nose-down sense. No tendency to drop a wing or spin from the stall has been encountered.

Spinning tests have been conducted with characteristics similar to the F-102. Neither aircraft would recover with forward stick, and will recover satisfactorily only with neutral stick and rudder, and pro-spin aileron. The XF-106 loses approximately 4000 ft per turn, and tests were delayed at one time after the need on one occasion to use the anti-spin chute for recovery.

Sixteen aircraft have been flown in the development programme to date, and none of these has a representative production cockpit. Difficulties have been experienced with the development of the MA1 Hughes Weapons System (it seems that an alternative weapons system is also under development at Wright ADC) and that the final production cockpit configuration has yet to be decided. In this connection there was general agreement that whatever the outcome the operational machine would have the twin grip stick as used in the F-102; and that immediately forward of this would be a Hughes ground position indicator (GPI) presentation. This would present TACAN information as a dot on a map, the dot indicating the aircraft's actual position at any time. (This equipment seems to be precisely what is needed in this country for fighter navigation.)

The airbrakes were satisfactory up to existing limits, and produced no buffet. They were also described as no more powerful relatively than those of an F-86; and Mr Johnson said that when used over small deflections (they are variable) a measurable improvement in Nv (directional stability) is obtained supersonically.

Wheelbrakes are pedal-operated without auto-braking, and it was stated that these are smooth and satisfactory in operation, although it was generally agreed that for marginal operation on surfaces giving poor coefficient of friction auto-braking would be desirable.

The cambered leading edge, introduced with the Series 20 wing, had improved stability and general handling considerably throughout the whole flight envelope. This was most apparent to the pilot as an altitude gain subsonically in manoeuvre, and as improved controllability on the approach and landing. This has been obtained at the expense of a small increase in supersonic wave-drag.

Originally two chordwise fences had been fitted to the F-106, but these had been eliminated in favour of small chordwise leading-edge slots which did the job effectively, and with less drag than the fences. (Investigation subsequently showed that these slots were of similar dimensions and in similar positions relative to the leading edge span as those on the P.1.)

Flutter clearance had been carried out to 750 kt without delay and without difficulty. Flight resonance tests had been conducted with a 'variable eccentric' device, covering the full range of flutter modes. They had no knowledge or experience of the explosive charge method. Provision is made in the design for flight refuelling, and underwing ferry tanks will be carried.

No data was obtainable on landing distance in unfavourable conditions, and landing measurements on flooded or icy runways had not yet been made and are scheduled to begin later this year. Col Lane had made one landing on a runway flooded after a heavy shower and, after rolling to 6000 ft with drag chute on, had experienced a slide sideways of 200–300 ft while attempting to turn off on the wet surface. It was stated that idling thrust on the J79 will maintain 83 kt indefinitely under zero wind conditions on a level runway.

In rain, vision through the vee windscreen with windscreen blow was described as relatively good and certainly much better with blowing than without.

The double stick which has been well liked on the F-102 will be retained on the - 106, but difficulties are experienced in obtaining adequate throw in the lateral sense as the inside of the leg limits stick travel.

The turn co-ordinator should be selected 'ON' throughout (this provides rudder input to counter adverse yaw).

Pattern speeds:

Join at 310 kt with eighty-four per cent throttle. 240 kt: lower undercarriage and stabilise. Final approach at 185 kt/eighty-eight per cent. Hold-off, 160–155 kt for touchdown at approximately 140 kt.

The ejection seat fitted was the standard Stanley seat with rocket catapult. This is a 'one motion' ejection seat with a minimum altitude capability with auto-parachute of approximately 2000 ft. Before reaching this height prior to landing, the parachute D-ring is disconnected from 'Auto' and made Manual to enable (in theory) manual separation and development at low altitude.

Flight Report No. 7
Convair Experimental/Edwards AFB, California

Aircraft:	F-106A No. 6453
Engine:	J75-9 (unmodified)
Date:	30 June 1958
Weight:	31,000 lb
CG:	twenty-eight per cent aerodynamic mean chord
Fuel:	8000 lb (7800 lb indicated)
Special limitations:	Mach 1.5 indicated, with intake slotted ramps de-activated
Flight time:	forty-five minutes

Cockpit layout, dimensions and drill were almost indentical with those of the F-102A, with the exception that electrical controls had been regrouped and slightly simplified.

A canopy locking warning light was fitted to the main panel and on the first and second attempts at locking, this light remained on. It was finally extinguished by operating the manual locking handle with great vigour.

Engine checks prior to taxying: Fifty-seven per cent, 310°C, oil pressure forty-three pounds per square inch. All systems normal, all warning lights out.

Taxying control was improved over the F-102, with less coarse nosewheel steering gear ratio; and on the extended taxying to runway 04 in the intense heat at Edwards, it was pleasant to be able to lock the canopy in the half-open position with the locking switch provided immediately forward of the manual raising handle.

After checking ratiometer setting with Convair radio, the short pre-take-off check list was completed, maximum cold power set against the brakes, and reheat nozzle position checked. With the stopwatch at zero, the brakes were released and reheat was lit with only a small delay after simple rotation of the throttle, outboard. With reheat functioning smoothly, the throttle was advanced to maximum power and the resulting acceleration rate was felt to be rather less than that of a P.1B in cold thrust at similar weight (but at UK temperatures).

Directional control of the initial take-off run was good using nosewheel steering, and on rotating into nosewheel lift at the briefed 120 kt the relative lightness of the elevon was unexpected and the unstick occurred quickly, though quite smoothly. Immediately after becoming airborne, lightness of the controls in pitch and roll was apparent but not as over-sensitivity.

The undercarriage was selected up at approximately 170 kt and was retracted fully by 200 kt. As with the F-102, it was necessary to grope round the outer side of the throttle to reach and operate the undercarriage selector lever which was easily visible at all times.

After a short check for acceleration, a shallow climb-away was initiated which was steepened on reaching 500 kt IAS. (Total fuel indicated at take-off: 6850 lb. Engine speed: ninety-eight per cent. Altimeter setting: 29.8 millibars).

HEIGHT (AMSL)	SPEED	TIME
20,000 ft	Mach .88	Zero+2.20 min
30,000 ft	Mach .9	Zero+2.55 min
40,000 ft	Mach .89	Zero+3.42 min

Control of the climb was smooth and accurate, with response in pitch and roll harmonised nicely, and little or no adverse yaw in aileron turns. At no time did the climb angle approach that experienced at maximum power on the P.1B.

Cabin conditioning had been set as briefed in the auto range, and no readjustments were required during this climb as the cockpit temperature was maintained at a comfortable level throughout.

With maximum reheat maintained, a turn to port was initiated at 41,000 ft at approximately 1.6 g, and held through 210 degrees before straightening out. During this turn the ASI system jump-up occurred at 40,500 ft. A level acceleration was recorded while maintaining max reheat power at 98.2 per cent/595°C.

HEIGHT (AMSL)	SPEED	TIME
39,000 ft	Mach 1.1	Zero+5.30 min (Total fuel: 4000 lb)
39,000 ft	Mach 1.23	Zero+6 min
39,500 ft	Mach 1.31	Zero+6.30 min
40,000 ft	Mach 1.4	Zero+7 min (Total fuel: 3400 lb)

At Mach 1.43 with acceleration continuing at the same rate, 2 g was pulled and maintained in a climbing turn to port. On passing through 45,000 ft, speed had dropped to Mach 1.2 indicated after turning through approximately ninety degrees. (Total indicated fuel: 3200 lb.)

Power was cut from maximum reheat to maximum cold, and this occurred with a slight thump and fluctuation of the engine gauges. The wrist movement throttle action for this operation was well liked.

A left-rudder-induced, stick-free, dutch roll at Mach 1.08 indicated/1 g was damped visually in 2.5 cycles. These tests were carried out with all dampers 'IN' and with turn co-ordinator, and this damping rate was therefore a slight deterioration over that experienced at a similar flight condition in the F-102A which had damping to deadbeat in ½ cycle transonically with dampers 'IN'. As in original transition at 40,000 ft after the climb, control responses and trim changes in transition between Mach 1.0–0.9 indicated were exceptionally good, with very little trim reversal or variation being detectable in 1 g flight, and only small changes under 1.5 g conditions. (Trim co-ordinator inoperative).

Within this speed range the elevon trim actuator operated jerkily in the longitudinal sense, and it was not easy to trim out precisely at the transition point of approximately Mach 0.98 indicated. Owing to briefed engine handling restrictions, maximum cold power had to be maintained while speed was being reduced. However, momentarily forgetting this restriction while passing through 27,000 ft in a 2.5 g turn to port at about Mach 0.85 indicated, I reduced power smoothly to seventy-five per cent and at this point a muffled explosive condition occurred which gave a pressure system pulse through the cabin conditioning system. A check with Convair radio confirmed that this was a compressor stall which was to be expected in this flight condition; but, as no flame-out or other disturbance resulted, no further attention was given to this condition beyond the required increase in engine speed while at altitude.

At Zero + 15 min, 20,000 ft, total fuel indicated was 3000 lb. After checks of all service and warning systems which were normal, handling checks were continued at subsonic speed.

At approximately 20,000 ft/400 kt IAS the buffet threshold was found at 2.5 g, and in manoeuvre below Mach 0.9 indicated, in the range Mach 0.9–0.85, control response and damping on all axes was excellent, with forces light and harmony very good; longitudinal control being heavier than lateral, just sufficient to give good harmony.

Some radio difficulty with a sticking channel selector was experienced at this stage, and so a precautionary return to circuit was made, slightly earlier than intended.

The circuit was joined with 2300 lb total fuel, and control under circuit conditions from 300–350 kt IAS was entirely straightforward.

Lowering the undercarriage downwind at 250 kt, little trim change occurred and undercarriage lowering was associated with two small jolts. Locking down occurred in approximately eight seconds. The pattern was carried out at the briefed speeds without difficulty, and with little adverse yaw in rough air; the final turn being made at eighty-eight per cent cold power and approximately 200 kt without any sign of approaching the buffet boundary. While following the aircraft ahead (a Lockheed Jetstar prototype) the initial Finals were made rather too high, and on correction the approach speed was slightly higher than briefing, about 190 kt reducing to 180 kt using eighty-eight per cent power. Control of the glide path in pitch and direction was good, and no difficulty was experienced in correcting the original error.

With power set at approximately eighty-five per cent, the roundout was begun over the runway threshold at 168 kt, and this resulted in an easy flare-out and short float before touching down gently at around 140 kt IAS.

Conclusions

The basic characteristics of the XF-106 are similar to those of the F-102 as are the systems and cockpit layout, and it was possible to make some attempt at measuring performance from the start on this one flight.

From this limited experience it was clear that the F-106 contained many control features which were developments from and improvements on the F-102 production standard. In particular, transition trim changes had been reduced (stabilisers 'IN') to insignificant proportions; and clearly the turn co-ordinator takes care of the adverse yaw characteristics which are quite apparent on the F-102.

The result is a pleasantly-balanced aircraft which is easy to control and pleasant to fly throughout the limited conditions experienced.

Performance, which during the climb phase promises well, is disappointing at altitude and, as measured, does not approach the standard at present achieved with the P.1B series.

The high rate of fuel consumption rather offsets the 7800 lb indicated fuel on start-up, and with total production fuel it seems that the P.1B is lilely to be quite as well off in this respect.

Seat comfort and control layout in the cockpit were good, but forward vision through the Convair V-windscreen was found to be very restricting. It can be said, therefore, that at the present time on the F-106 a high standard of artificial stability and control has been achieved; and that, in its present form, the aircraft is already likely to be suitable for all-weather operation up to and including supersonic speeds.

No information was available on the present timescale of the ultimate weapons system, but it was clear that much work remains to be done on the intake/engine installation to recover design performance, before a production configuration with a specification performance can be achieved.

Although limited by the current engine and intake development problems, it was clear that the handling qualities of this second generation, delta-wing fighter were already excellent and likely to result in a practical and formidable Mach 2 all-weather fighter, when the specified power became available.

It seemed likely also that the Hughes MA1 weapons system would provide some advantages over the Ferranti AirPass system of the Lightning. However, the Lightning was likely to remain superior on many counts. These included acceleration and time to altitude, and hard-turning capability and sustained g at all altitudes due to the Lightning's low-tailplane configuration which produced significantly less lift-loss and induced drag in the turn than did the all-elevon delta wing of the XF-106. Also, the Lightning's inherant stability was a marked safety and reliability factor, in contrast to the auto-stabiliser-dependent XF-106 (on all axes).

So this interesting visit to the centre of American military test flying ended on a high note, with the sheer enjoyment of landing this fine new fighter easily and without complication on the wide expanse of Edwards AFB, under the brilliant afternoon sky.

However, on the way back to the UK it was also pleasant to reflect that in the Lightning it was now clear that the RAF had a fighter which could handle anything in the USAF's inventory up to and including the F-106.

Over the next three decades both aircraft justified those predictions and gained great reputations among succeeding generations of fighter pilots. The F-106 was still equipping squadrons of the Air National Guard in 1988, and was finally phased out of service in that year. Lightnings continued in front-line defence of the UK until June 1988 at Binbrook, where the pilots of Nos. 5 and 11 Squadrons claimed that they could 'still see off anything we meet in the skies of Europe'. They had albums of recording camera shots of 'bounced' F-16s, F-15s, Mirages and F-5s to prove it — 'and F-4s, of course, have never been a problem'!

Of the first three generations of subsonic, transonic, and Mach 2-capable jet fighters, the North American F-86 Sabre was undoubtedly the classic of the first era. The English Electric Lightning will always be held, by its pilots at least, to be the finest of the first Mach 2 fighters, the F-106 and Mirage running it close in all departments except combat manoeuvrability in which the Lightning was supreme.

Shortly after this fascinating experience of flying the best USAF supersonic fighters, a team of test pilots and engineers from the Edwards Air Force Base test centre came to the English Electric Company's test airfield at Warton to evaluate the Lightning; and Majors 'Deke' Slayton (later famous as manager of the Apollo astronauts) and 'Bud' Anderson expressed lively appreciation of the qualities of the British Mach 2 fighter.

Some years later an instructor from the USAF's Interceptor Weapons School, on an exchange posting to the Fighter Command Trials Unit at RAF Binbrook, reported on the Lightning Mk 6:

Capt Dan Schuyller
USAF Interceptor Weapons School
Hooray! Hooray! The first of May turned out to be good news day!

Last May I had much to shout about because it was my very good fortune to spend a remote one-month TDY in England. My fellow traveller was Major Don Parkhurst from the Test Squadron. Our hosts were members of FCTU (Fighter Command Trials Unit — counterpart of our Test Squadron) located at RAF Binbrook.

We visited [the] RAF Coltishall (CCTS) and RAF Valley (where their firing programme is conducted separate form FCTU). Our purpose was to fly the English Electric Lightning, England's best interceptor, and then talk about it. I have never flown a more impressive airplane, nor been treated with more genuine hospitality. I shall attempt to explain my reaction to the airplane.

Aircraft
The airplane handles like an F-86 with the power of the F-101. It is an extremely honest and forgiving airplane throughout the flight envelope from Mach .25 to Mach 2 plus. It is very stable in the GCA pattern, and at high speeds (1.6 plus) it turns at high G (4) with little or no airspeed loss. I will discuss later how this feature is put to work tactically. The maximum range profile is 800NM, but in-flight refuelling allows a range dictated only by PPS (pilot posterior sensitivity).

The take-off was thrilling on each of my seventeen trips — like Zoomar! 31,800 pounds of thrust plus 38,000 pounds of Lightning equals 210 pounds of nervous energy!

Climb is made in military power (24,600 pounds of thrust) at 450 knots to best cruise altitude of 36,000 ft — time elapsed from brake release is about 3.30 minutes. Failure to come out of burner would result in passing through 36,000 ft after 1.45 minutes — that is if you remembered to raise the gear and flaps.

When it is time to RTB the power is brought to idle/idle (yes, it has two Rolls-Royce engines cleverly disguised by using a common intake and mounting them vertically — only one aircrew, though), the speed brakes extended and a plunge towards the ground is begun at 375 kt. Need I mention that [your] 'block altitude' is dictated only be the limits of the airplane. Traffic pattern and landing speeds are nearly identical to those of the F-106.

An interesting feature while on the ground is the wheel brakes. They are controlled by a lever on the stick; hence, all Lightning pilots have a firm, well-controlled handshake.

Radar
The radar is quite unsophisticated, refreshingly so in fact, and is very adequate to

fire the externally mounted IR missiles in the stern; however, front firings of the armament could be a bit shaky against an ECM or chaff target due to fire control system limitations.

One fascinating feature of the fire control system is called kinematic ranging. Where we use a known altitude differential and a known antenna train angle to manually angle range, a Lightning pilot has an automatic firing capability, using the same principle but different known quantities. The computer uses interceptor Mach, target Mach and antenna rate of movement to fire the armament at the proper range. At present it is about as reliable as our IR range computer, but I feel it has a much greater possibility to be developed into a valuable aid, because it uses more realistic known quantities. Not as exciting as the price of oranges in Texas, perhaps, but you might think about the feasibility of adapting this principle to your aircraft — automatic fire in IR dominant, radar passive mode.

Armament
The IR missiles on the airplane are most impressive — adequate thrust to give a large firing area between minimum and maximum launch; a very discriminating seeker head that allows accurate proximity as well as contact fuzing, and, best of all, a missile that cannot be launched until it 'sees' the target. This latest feature enables the pilot to have an excellent manual firing capability against a difficult target ie, ECM, chaff, low altitude, manoeuvring etc.

The pilot must position the aircraft so that the missile 'sees' the target which is indicated by the illumination of lights. (A headset tone would help here against a fighter target so that the pilot could keep his opponent in sight at all times). After the missile acquires the target, the remaining task is to put the target within the firing bracket and then hose away.

The optical sight may be used as an aid both in missile acquisition and in determination of proper firing range. The beauty of the sight is its wide field of view. Would you believe, the entire windscreen? The pilot must find another spot to hand his helmet — no immovable telescope with a 5.75 degree field of view.

Tactics
Two of the main factors in determining tactic selection are target speed and interceptor armament. The Firestreak missile must be fired in the stern quarter. The tactic used with this missile is similar to our single offset stern. When approaching in the front quarter the attack geometry corresponds to our double offset stern without the J-leg. At offset the turn is made with forty-five degrees angle of bank subsonic, and sixty degrees supersonic. Airspeed control in this turn is a joy to behold due to the excess thrust available. This is true even with ninety-degree bank high 'G' turns.

The tactic used with the Red Top missile is basically a cut-off attack if the target speed is great enough to allow a front IR firing. The front attack requires a radar lock-on, either a range or an angle lock-on will suffice. If both are denied then a re-attack is made, allowing very little target travel because of the outstanding manoeuvrability and acceleration of the Lightning. This capability was one of the most impressive features of the Lightning. It allowed a novice like me to stumble, fumble and fall on the front attack, but to salvage the re-attack in minimum time with an assist from a G suit.

Intercept techniques
The one thing that stands out concerning intercept techniques is the pilot's ability to transform what he sees on the scope, prior to lock-on, into a mental picture of

the attack geometry. If the picture is a bleak one then he takes immediate action to make it more to his liking.

This ability is not a gift from the blue but the result of a great deal of effort in the simulator (crazy motion simulators that actually work) and in the air against unknown targets. The controller gives the target range and bearing, and the pilot earns his pay.

The procedure used to complete the intercept is not a simple one, but it works very nicely. The end result in training of this type is that the pilots are well equipped to operate in an environment without GCI control.

Hooray! Horray!

I hope you can see why I am so entralled with the Lightning — it goes fast, turns spectacularly, has good IR armament and is a distinct pleasure to fly.

You have undoubtedly noticed that I have not mentioned any of the drawbacks of the aircraft. There are few, I suppose — no IR search and track system, no radar missile, no all weather capability against ECM and chaff. I can't help but wonder, if it had all these features, whether or not it would still go fast etc.

I feel that the Lightning can do one job more certainly than any aircraft. I know I would leap at the chance to fly it again but I've probably already used up my 'good deal' cards for this year — come May of '67 though: Hooray! Horray!

By the mid-1960s it was clear that Britain had closed its self-imposed gap in supersonic technology, and, indeed, had come out ahead with the most combat-manoeuvrable, Mach 2, all-weather, fighter in the world.

Chapter Six
Testing the First British Supersonic Bomber, TSR2

In the 1950s British aviation had made a major stride forward to a leading position in supersonics with the successful English Electric P.1, P.1B and Lightning; and the delta wing Fairy FD.2 which reached 1000 mph after the P.1 in 1956, and went on to establish the official world's absolute speed record in excess of 1000 mph for the first time.

   This progress was then arrested sharply by the 1957 Government's White Paper on Defence ('the Sandys storm'), which appeared to forecast the end of military supersonic aircraft in the UK and their substitution, in all future roles of defence

The British Aircraft Corporation TSR2, serial XR219, being prepared for its first flight, Boscombe Down, September 1964. *(British Aerospace)*

and attack, by rocket missiles. It announced also the cancellation of the existing requirement for a supersonic bomber replacement for the Canberra.

That this philosophy was seriously faulted was recognised within two years however. Confidence in the future of British supersonics was renewed when Operational Requirement GOR 339 was confirmed in January 1959. The aircraft, which would be called TSR.2, would be a large, multi-role, highly supersonic, strike and reconnaissance aircraft, filling most of the roles of the existing Canberra and V-bomber fleets; and would keep the RAF in a position of technical and operational superiority into the last decades of the century and onwards, with periodic updating, into the twenty-first century.

The requirement was stringent and called for state-of-the-art aerodynamics, structures, engines (for supersonic cruise), avionics and, in particular, weapons systems; to such an extent that the MoD granted a contract for it only on condition that at least two of the major aircraft manufacturers merged into one 'consortium', the Ministry considering that none of the existing companies would have the capacity to bring such a demanding programme to a successful conclusion alone.

After much consultation within the Industry, English Electric, Vickers and Bristol agreed to form a combined company which became, in 1960, the British Aircraft Corporation (and subsequently British Aerospace in the 1980s). BAC was contracted to design, develop and build fifty TSR.2 aircraft for the RAF, with the expectation from the beginning that Australia would also have a requirement for twenty or more.

The specification was complex and, by November 1962, required:

Two Bristol-Siddeley Olympus 22R Mk 320 twin-spool, axial flow engines with water injection and variable reheat and designed for sustained cruise at Mach 2+, each giving 19,600 lb ST dry and 30,610 lb ST reheat (ISA).

Total internal fuel:	5588 imp gals
Ferry tanks:	2400 imp gals
Flight refuelling:	400 gals/min
Maximum cruise speed at 200 ft:	Mach 0.9 (1.1 over target)
Maximum cruise speed above 36,000 ft:	Mach 2.05
Vne:	800 KIAS
Design Maximum Mach No.:	2.75 (limiting recovery temp 146°C)
Maximum operating altitude:	54,000 ft
Radius of Action (with ten per cent Mach 1.7 above 40,000 ft, and twenty per cent at Mach 0.9 at 200 ft, and with one 2000 lb store/ internal):	1850 kms
(or all, at Mach 0.9 at 200 ft):	1286 kms
Ferry range (with drop tanks):	6850 kms
Take-off ground roll at T/O weight 95,000 lbs:	915 ms
Max T/O weight:	105,000 lb (with growth potential to over 120,000 lb)

Armament (initial configuration):	Internal weapons bay, 20 ft, with 1 nuclear or 6×1000 lb HE. Four wing pylons for 4× 1000 lb HE, or 4×37 rocket packs, or nuclears on inner pylons only.

Dimensions
span:	37 ft
length:	86 ft
height:	23 ft 5 in
wing area:	700 sq ft
Aspect ratio:	1:96

The 60° swept wing was designed specifically for low gust response and had full span 'blown' flaps with lateral control by differential tailplane 'Tailerons'.

The navigation/attack system depended upon Doppler and inertia sensors, with a navigation computer using heading data from the IP and Doppler, and drift from the IP.

Fixing from sidways-looking radar (Linescan) corrected heading and position error.

Forward-looking radar linked into the nav system for terrain following and, in addition, had modes for radar-ranging (dive attack), ground-mapping, homing on tanker aircraft, and limited search capability over sea or areas of low ground clutter.

System accuracy requirements included 'blind' delivery to less than 100 ft error at more than 1000 nm with radar fixes every 100 nm, the last at 30 nm from the target.

Flight trials of the prototype, XR219, began in 1964 with extensive runway testing at the BAC 'field' test base at Boscombe Down; and the TSR.2 took off for the first time on 27 September, as described in the author's flight report:

British Aircraft Corporation (Operating) Ltd
Preston Division
Experimental Flight Report No. 1
Date:	27 September 1964
Aircraft type:	TSR.2
serial no.:	XR.219
Object of test:	Initial flight at Boscombe Down
Pilot:	R. P. Beamont
Navigator:	D. J. Bowen
Test configuration:	Undercarriage extended. Auxiliary air intake doors locked open. Intake cones 'fixed'.

Take-off loading
Fuel (indicated contents)
Forward group:	9050 lb
No. 2 tank:	3000 lb
Aft group:	6550 lb
No. 4 tank:	2000 lb
Total indicated fuel:	15,600 lb

Fuel
usable:	16,151 lb
unusable:	1687 lb
total:	17,838 lb

Tare weight and equipment:	58,098 lb
Crew:	340 lb
LOX	24 lb
Total take-off weight:	76,300 lb
Take-off time:	15.28 hr
Landing time:	15.42 hr
Total flight time:	0.14 hr
C.G. position at take-off:	21.6 in AOD (39.8 per cent SMC) U/C down.
Engines	
type:	Bristol-Siddeley Olympus 320X
serial no. 1:	22218
serial no. 2:	22221

Alterations since taxi test 11:
1. Turn round inspection carried out.
2. Aircraft refuelled to Load Sheet 219/3, Case C.
3. Ref. Pilot's query: 'Stbd. forward brake indicating 2000 psi'. This has been accepted for first flight.

XR219 in high drag configuration during an early test flight, with the full-span 'blown' flaps at fifty degrees and airbrakes at the maximum deflection, fifty-five degrees. *(British Aerospace)*

Cockpit checks completed to Flight Reference Cards, Issue 3 amended.

Fuel on entry:	F. 9200/A. 6400 lb
C.G:	39.0 per cent (G)
	39.2 per cent (F)
Undercarriage indicators:	Three greens, nosewheel red
Brake accumulators:	3200/3000 psi
Parking brakes:	1500/1600 psi
	1500/1600 psi

H.D.D. Attitude Indicator, two degrees port bank error

Main altimeter set:	1013.2 mbs
Oxygen:	Full/95 psi
Air Data Test:	1. 6450 ft
	2. 45,100 ft

Engine starts

No. 1:	33 per cent/400°C–35 secs
	58.2 per cent/310°C–1.15 min
No. 2:	No cycle at first. After discussion with Flight Test Van it was decided to re-cycle, and this second attempt was satisfactory: 56.2 per cent/294°C
Brake accumulators:	4200/4000 psi

Hydraulic services

No. 1 controls:	3500 psi
No. 2 controls:	3500 psi
No. 1 services:	3600 psi
No. 2 services:	3700 psi

Cabin air selected from manual to full auto cool, and high flow conditions occurred at 70/70 per cent which persisted for two-three minutes before reducing to normal.

During the high flow condition the use of the shut-off cock was investigated, and it was confirmed that this cut off airflow into the cabin after approximately thirty seconds. The cock was returned to normal and power increased to above 70 per cent N_h, where flow conditions were found to have returned to normal with a comfortable cabin temperature.

It was decided to continue the sortie on the basis that if an unacceptably high flow rate was encountered in flight, it could be eliminated by use of the shut-off cock.

Reheat checks

No. 1:	99 per cent/680°C, first gutter light-up, satisfactory
No. 2:	99 per cent/685°C, first gutter light-up, satisfactory

Loud crackling background and distorted reception were experienced on UHF Channel 3 with ground stations and the chase aircraft, and this was isolated to the upper aerial. Radio conditions on lower aerial were satisfactory.

Take-Off

The aircraft was lined up on Runway 24 with all systems serviceable.

Wind:	290 degrees/11 kt

Ground level ambient
   temperature: +18.2°C
Altimeter: 1013.2 mb

After burning off and balancing, fuel was adjusted to 13,300 lb, differential 8000/5300 lb, for take-off.

Brake temperature: 50/50°C
Maximum dry intermediate: 98.5 per cent/690°C
                              97.5 per cent/698°C

Flaps thirty-five degrees, 'blow' in mid-thirty-five degree segment.

Reset to flaps 20°, 'blow' in mid-20° segment.

Nosewheel steering, FINE gear.

Reheat lights to third gutter, satisfactory.

Runway acceleration normal.

Initial rotation at 125 kt, and nosewheel checked between one and two ft.

Rotation continued at 170 kt with lift-off occurring with buffet vibration at approximately 180 kt (CSI).

In slight crosswind conditions a small lateral correction was required and achieved.

Acceleration in the initial climb-out was slow, and attitude was corrected at about 500 ft in order to establish 200 kt before resuming the climb incidence necessary to hold 200 kt at maximum reheat.

From 1000 ft speed was increased gradually to 240 kt, and reheat cancelled at approximately 3000 ft with unevenness through the gutters.

Buffet was present throughout this phase, of moderate amplitude and predominantly 4-5 cycles lateral at the cockpit.

On climb: 5000 ft, 220 kt, 97.7/97.2 per cent, 696/698°C.

During the intitial climb-out phase the attitude developed was such that forward vision was lost, and the seat was raised to establish forward view. The seat raising switch was conveniently placed and easy to use in this situation.

Normal Flight

Level flight was established at 6500 ft and a rate .5 port turn set up beginning at 93/93 per cent and increasing to 96/96 per cent to sustain.

On levelling out, 35 degrees flap was selected and produced a nose-down trim change of three to four pounds' stick force. As the incidence changed with flap, the buffet level was reduced but not eliminated.

Response in roll and pitch was assessed at 220 kt in this configuration, and pitch damping was dead-beat; roll damping was low and subject to the effects of inertia. It was established that control in pitch and roll was adequate for gentle manoeuvres.

Control inputs in yaw and co-ordinated control movements resulted in relatively low response rates but otherwise normal response with some adverse yaw from the roll inputs, and speed was reduced as scheduled to 180 kt in the landing configuration (thirty-five degrees' flap).

Buffet continued down to 180 kt where it increased in amplitude slightly, and the chase Lightning reported 172 kt. This was accepted as evidence of possible adverse position error, and adjustments were made to the minimum speeds selected for the remainder of the sortie.

180 kt CSI was sustained in level flight in the landing configuration at thirty-five degrees' flap (and 'blow') at 7,000 ft, with 94/94 per cent N_h. Up to this point re-trimming had not been required on any axis.

A gentle descent was set up at 80/80 per cent achieving 250 kt passing 5,000 ft, and buffet amplitude remained as before. It was confirmed that the predominant characteristic was a four to five cycle lateral mode with some higher frequency background.

At the planned point in the first circuit, review of the state of fuel and general systems serviceability confirmed that the second scheduled circuit was practical, and this was confirmed by radio.

The base leg turn was completed at 3000 ft, 210 kt, and it was a simple matter to line up and establish the approach path, though a slight tendency to chase the glide slope was noticed due to low pitch response rate and light feel force.

Overshoot was initiated from 1700 ft at 'maximum dry intermediate', and an adequate though small climb rate established before retracting flap to twenty degrees.

On levelling out for the downwind leg, a left rudder, stick-free, dutch roll was carried out at 240 kt, flaps twenty degrees, developing approximately forty-five degrees port bank with damping to half amplitude in approximately two cycles and two seconds.

A stick jerk in similar conditions produced low rate but adequate response in pitch, with damping dead-beat in one cycle.

Flaps thirty-five degrees selected for a PE check at 2000 ft; CSI 201 kt — Lightning 199 kt.

Landing

The aircraft was turned on to base leg at Thruxton as planned (five-and-a-half miles from the threshold of runway 24), and lined up easily at 1500 ft/190 kt CSI; and the centre-line and glide slope were maintained relatively easily, though with inertia affecting positive precision in roll and a very slight tendency to over-controlling in pitch, again due to low response rate and light feel force.

Final adjustments to landing attitude at short finals including a check in flare response were satisfactory. The threshold was crossed at 190 kt CSI/100 ft, and power reduced very slightly during positive flare initiation at approximately 180 kt. Control of dry engine power was adequate for approach speed adjustment in the prevailing favourable conditions.

As predicted the change in attitude was positive but the effect on the glide slope small, though sufficient to reduce the rate of decent at contact to a low value.

The rear main wheels were felt to touch smoothly at 500–600 yd from the threshold as planned, wings level and without detectable drift; and immediately after contact two to three cycles of heavy amplitude undercarriage/structural vibration was felt (wind 290 degrees/15 kt). Power was reduced to idle/idle, and the undercarriage vibration was eliminated apparently as the forward main wheels touched; the nose was allowed to descend gently into contact with the runway with little forward movement of the stick.

At nosewheel contact the speed was down to approximately 155 kt, and the tail parachute handle operated. After a relatively lengthy pause development was felt, and subsequent de-reefing produced a powerful, smooth deceleration.

The landing was made with nosewheel steer engaged and no sharp steering effects were noted. It should, however, be practical to delay nosewheel steer to low speeds in future.

As landing roll conditions were entirely smooth and satisfactory use of wheel braking was delayed to approximately 100 kt, and this resulted in brake temperatures registering only 80/80°C at standstill. Accumulator pressures 4000/4000 psi.

The tail parachute was jettisoned normally at approximately 20 kt. Fuel 5100/2900 lb. Wind 280°/13-15 kt.

The navigator reported that the starboard undercarriage bogie rotation may not have been fully complete at the touchdown point, which could have led to the vibration condition experienced.

Cockpit temperatures high throughout the sortie with 'Auto Full Cold' selected.

After taxying back, shut-down checks:

58.5 per cent/314°C:	57 per cent/294°C
Brake temperatures:	180/300°C
Brake accumulators:	4100/4200 psi

Summary

Due to virtually complete serviceability this first sortie was carried out in full accordance with Flight Test Schedule No. 1.

Stability and response to controls was found to be adequate and safe for flight under the conditions tested, and to conform closely to predicted and simulated values.

Noticeably high induced drag was experienced after take-off, due possibly to adverse position error resulting in too early lift-off.

Moderate amplitude buffet was experienced at all speeds tested, and this was found to vary in amplitude with incidence.

Control of the approach and landing was especially excellent having regard to the current absence of auto-stabilisation.

Engine control and behaviour was adequate at all points in the flight, except in disengagement of reheat during the climb-out where the usual difficulty was experienced in throttle-box disengagement of minimum reheat.

Engine speed adjustment of the approach was not faulted, but it should be noted that the prevailing weather conditions on the approach were non-turbulent.

All supporting systems functioned perfectly, with the exception of the temperature and flow control of cabin conditioning which tended to pulse throughout the sortie and was too warm.

The warning system functioned satisfactorily, and no spurious warnings occurred. Fuel balancing was not required during flight, and fuel system performance was not faulted.

Cockpit layout was satisfactory with some exceptions. The forward windscreen and instrument shroud layout were particularly excellent and virtually no significant reflections were seen in the glasses in spite of the intense sun-glare during approach and landing. The canopy transparencies were of very low vision quality.

In general, the performance, stability and response to controls conformed closely to the briefed values and especially to the simulator studies. Virtually all scheduled test points were achieved on the flight and this, coupled with the high standard of systems serviceability and the adequate level of un-auto-stabilised control and stability in this high drag, low-speed configuration, reflects a very high standard of design, preparation and inspection.

In this configuration and under the conditions tested, this aircraft could be flown safely by any moderately experienced pilot qualified on Lightning or similar aircraft, and the flight development programme can therefore be seen to be off to a good start.

It is clear that the current engine ratings leave the aircraft critically short of thrust, and this situation is lilkely to dictate the rate of flight development.

Defects
1. Cabin conditioning temperature and flow control unstable.
2. Canopy jettison handle safety-pin on floor of navigator's cockpit (in console).
3. Upper UHF aerial unserviceable.
4. Two degree bank error on pilot's HDD atitude indicator.

Following this successful first flight, essential undercarriage and engine development work delayed the second flight until the end of December; and then a series of undercarriage sequencing faults prevented early expansion of the flight envelope until, on the tenth flight, the undercarriage was retracted successfully.

British Aircraft Corporation (Operating) Ltd
Preston Division
Experimental Flight Report No. 10

Date:	6 February 1965
Aircraft type:	TSR.2
serial no.:	XR.219
Object of test:	Undercarriage cycling and extension of limits
Pilot:	R. P. Beamont
Navigator:	D. J. Bowen

Take-off loading

Fuel (indicated contents)	
Forward group:	10,550 lb
No. 2 tank:	3700 lb
Aft group:	8050 lb
No. 4 tank:	2750 lb
Total ind fuel:	18,600 lb
Fuel	
usable:	19,151 lb
unusable:	1687 lb
total:	20,838 lb
Tare weight and equip:	58,371 lb
Crew:	340 lb
LOX:	24 lb
Total take-off weight:	79,573 lb
Flight no.:	Ten
Take-off time:	11.01 hr
Landing time:	11.30 hr
Total flight time:	0.29 hr
Time from start-up to shut down:	1.04 hr
C.G. position at take-off:	22 in AOD (40 per cent SMC U/C extended

Engines

type:	Bristol-Siddeley Olympus 320X
serial no. 1:	22210
serial no. 2:	22215

Pre-flight checks completed to Flight Reference Cards Issue 3, AL3.

Emergency oxygen:	1800 psi
Fuel:	F. 10600/A. 8100 lb
C.G:	G. 39.5 per cent
	F. 39.7 per cent

Undercarriage Indicator:	Nosewheel red light three green lights
Aileron gearing indicator:	Five degrees
Brake accumulators:	3100/2100 psi
Brakes:	F. 1400/1600 psi
	A. 1500/1400 psi
Altimeter zeros:	Standby 1028 mb
	Main 1024 mb
Heading Indicator checks:	Pilot 266
	Navigator 266
Auxiliary intake doors:	Closed/Closed
Oxygen:	Full/100 psi
Lower aerial:	Selected
ADC test:	1. 6450 ft
	2. 44,800 ft

Engine Starts

No. 1: During the starting cycle electrical power was lost, and this was found the be due to both generator switches being in the 'ON' position. The possibility of this occurring during pre-flight checks had been noted due to the generator switches' ambiguous presentation with the 'ON' positon being in the normal centre 'OFF' position and unlabelled.

No. 1 dry cycle completed before satisfactory start on the second attempt.

T5:	4.5 sec
Idle:	57.2 per cent/290°C
Auxiliary intake doors:	Open/closed

No. 2:

T5:	13.5 sec
30 per cent:	30.2 sec
Idle:	57.2 per cent/284°C
Auxiliary intake doors:	Open/open
Undercarriage indicator:	Three green lights
Brake accumulators:	4000/4000 psi
Cabin temperature controller:	Set to mid (normal)

Throughout the pre-flight checks and engine start the pilot's oxygen warning light had appeared at intervals (mask sealing correctly), and it was found that this could only be prevented by selecting Standby Regulator. It was decided to accept this condition for flight owing to the low altitude scheduled.

Compass heading checks:

Main:	240 degrees
E2B:	242 degrees

While taxying out at 60/60 per cent N_h the temperature in both cockpits became rather low (temperature controller 'Normal'), and the setting was increased to '¾ Warm'. This caused no perceptible increase in temperature during the next five minutes, and as the temperature level was becoming cold and uncomfortable, and as the sense operation of the system had become suspect over previous flights, the temperature selector was set back to '½ Cold'. After a few minutes this resulted in reduction in flow and a gradual increase in temperature. Later in the flight as temperature began to increase, the setting was increased to 'Normal' which maintained comfortable conditions for the remainder of the flight.

Engines set:	90/90 per cent
Nozzle over-ride checks:	Aj Shut/Shut

The classically clean lines of TSR2 are emphasised in this view taken during the twelfth test flight.
(British Aerospace)

Flap blow checks

Flap 20°:	Blow in mid-20° segment
Flap 35°:	Blow in mid-35° segment
Flap 50°:	Blow in mid-35° segment
Maximum Dry Intermediate:	98 per cent/730°C
	98 per cent/702°C
Auxiliary intake doors:	Open/Open
Flap:	20° selected
Aileron gearing indicator:	Ten degrees
Fuel:	F. 9600/ A. 6900 lb
C.G:	G. 39 per cent, F. 39.2 per cent

Take-off

Reheat lights satisfactory and staging to 3rd gutter.

Aj: Open/Open

Accleration normal with nosewheel lift initiated at 140 kt, and rotation from 170 kt to lift-off at 185 kt approximately.

Double Datum to Intermediate at 200 ft, and reheat cancelled at 1000 ft.

Weather deterioration had resulted in a cloud base varying from 1200–1800 ft, and the test point was set up under these restricted circumstances below cloud due to the current limitations on icing conditions and uncertainties in respect of performance of the Main Attitude and Heading Indicators.

After levelling at 1200 ft (Altimeter 1026 mb) IAS was reduced to 200 kt and undercarriage 'UP' selection made, wings level, at trimmed power. The 'UP' cycle occurred smoothly with little jolting and no significant trim change, and the light sequencing (recorded in the Navigator's report) appeared normal.

Without altering power setting speed began to increase with the gear up and flaps 20°, and while about to reduce speed a TCV.1 red warning occurred. This persisted for only two to four seconds and did not reappear. After discussion with the Flight Test Van it was decided to continue the sortie.

Airbrakes were operated briefly to reduce speed from 230–210 kt, and from trimmed condition at 200 kt, undercarriage 'DOWN' selection was made.

The cycle occurred with only minor jolting and no significant trim change. The light sequencing (recorded in the Navigator's report) was again normal, and the time to lock down also appeared to be normal. The resultant 'DOWN' sequences were reported to appear satisfactory by the chase aircraft.

It was noted that the auxiliary intake doors were Closed/Closed with undercarriage up, and re-set to Open/Open with undercarriage down.

Undercarriage 'UP' was selected at 200 kt/1800 ft, and again the cycle was normal and satisfactory. Auxiliary intake doors Closed/Closed.

Flaps zero were selected at 240 kt and a slight nose-up trim change noted, and speed allowed to increase slightly. On passing 270 kt a slight nose-down trimmer input was initiated and completed at 300 kt to stick-free trim.

The slight buffet remaining in the clean configuration at 270 kt had cleared by 280 kt, and flight conditions at 300 kt upwards remained completely smooth.

IAS was increased at altitude varying between 1200–2000 ft due to low cloud patches, and engine response checked at 350 kt.

At 350 kt/1500 ft No. 1 engine was throttled to 68 per cent N_h, and accelerated back to trim power with no adverse effect. This was repeated on No. 2 engine satisfactorily, and it was noted that at maximum asymmetry slight corresponding directional effects occurred which only required light pedal forces to hold slip-ball central.

On increasing IAS from 350–400 kt a further slight nose-down trim change was required. Flight conditions remained completely smooth at this point, and airbrakes were operated to full out with very little trim change (nose-down). Buffet vibration occurred from approximately one-third airbrake, and increased to moderate amplitude over the last five degrees (airbrake indicator). No directional trim change was noticeable.

Pitch control was responsive and well damped in this condition, and lateral control was rather more sensitive and less well damped, though still satisfactory.

IAS was increased to 500 kt/0.75 IMN, and a stick jerk recorded which produced very slight buffet vibration at maximum incidence and returned to approximately level attitude in one cycle. 86/96 per cent N_h.

In a 2 g turn approximately (accelerometer unserviceable) at 500–480 kt, pitch response and feel-force gradient were fully satisfactory; while lateral control was rather over-responsive, resulting in a slight tendency to over-control in roll.

In these manoeuvres there was no obvious variation in sideslip, and co-ordination of the slip indicator with rudder was not required.

At 450 kt/1800 ft a left and right rudder, stick-free, dutch roll was initiated with visual damping in approximately two-and-a-half cycles. The stick had to be regained before full completion of the motion, due to loss of height and the relatively low altitude.

Airbrakes full OUT were used to slow down, and drag on full extension at 450 kt was quite satisfactory for the flight condition.

At 400–430 kt a turn-in for a simulated low level attack run was made from the east of base, levelling out at 450 kt/100 ft and continuing for approximately two miles at approximately 100 ft with precise and perfectly damped control in pitch, and less well damped but adequate control in roll. Although moderate to quite heavy turbulence was reported by the chase aircraft, this was barely experienced in this aircraft and the qualities of stability and control at this speed and altitude were precise.

A turning climb-out to port was carried out at approximately 2 g reducing through buffet onset at 370 kt to 1 g at 230 kt, where twenty degree flaps were selected.

Undercarriage 'DOWN' was selected at trimmed power at 210 kt/1500 ft. This cycle was completed satisfactorily. Fuel: F. 6200/A. 3900 lb.

With airbrakes fully out and flaps thirty-five degrees, an approach was set up for an overshoot with 'Double Datum Normal' selected. Power conditions on the two degree approach at 200 kt appeared to be only slightly up on the standard case without airbrake, and on increasing to 'Max. Dry Normal' at 500 ft the overshoot was carried out with adequate power to spare.

Airbrakes were cycled four times at 220 kt/1000 ft on the downwind leg, and an approach set up for a fifty degree flap landing. The approach was stabilised at 180 kt at thirty-five degrees' flap, and fifty degrees selected at 200 yd finals and approximately 100 ft.

The slight nose-down trim change was corrected as in the previous landing, and approximately two cycles of longitudinal over-correct were initiated to assess response in this configuration close to the ground at approximately 170 kt. The final flare was held for a touchdown at 160 kt IAS, and this occurred at a slightly higher rate of descent than the previous three landings. Incidence: 14.5 degrees.

Immediately after touchdown a heavy lateral undercarriage/fuselage natural frequency oscillation occurred lasting approximately one second, and of approximately ±1.5 g amplitude lateral. This slightly delayed the intended immediate parachute stream, and when this was operated the nose was already commencing to lower. Development of the parachute increased the nose lowering rate, and as this was not checked with tailplane the vertical rate of descent of the nosewheel was greater than on previous landings, although not to an excessive degree.

The parachute was felt to develop to maximum de-reefed at once, and maximum wheel braking was intitiated and held on down to slow speed at the tail parachute jettison point. Immediately after this severe brake judder occurred. Brake temperatures: 400/250°C. Wind: 040°/15 kt. (Runway 06).

After touchdown the port bogies were felt to rise gently and the starboard wing dropped. No attempt was made to correct with lateral control on this occasion, but such correction should prove practical in high crosswind landings, if required. Landing roll, not recorded, approximately 800 yd.

Towards the latter end of the landing run, Pumps 1 and 4 warning captions were noted to flicker slightly, and while taxying in slowly this flickering became more persistent until, just prior to stopping at dispersal, the flickering had become a persistent warning. Increase of engine power did not alter this condition, and engines were shut down from 60/60 per cent.

Summary

Two complete cycles of undercarriage functioning were fully satisfactory at 200–210 kt. This was an unrepresentative speed for an 'UP' cycle, and was employed to provide the most favourable conditions for this first test. Satisfactory operation will require demonstration in the IAS range 210–240 kt for a practical climb-out.

In the clean configuration for the first time, the aircraft was found to be buffet-free in 1 g flight with the buffet boundary largely as predicted in the areas checked.

Pitch response and stability up to the current flutter limit of 500 kt IAS was found to be entirely satisfactory in this configuration (ie, without auto-stability).

Roll control was tending to become slightly over-sensitive at the highest IAS and may require some attention to gearing, although auto-stabilisation may be expected to improve this case. It was, however, satisfactory for continued extension of the flight envelope.

General flight conditions at 500 kt IAS in low cloud/moderate turbulence and low-level flying were extremely satisfactory and conducive to confidence; particularly at very low level where stability and well-matched damping and responsiveness in pitch added up to just the degree of precise control of the situation so essential for low-level combat.

The test confirmed immediately the control and stability qualities at high IAS, and was followed by another major step forward in the programme on 22 February 1965 when the prototype was flown from Boscombe Down in Wiltshire to Warton in Lancashire, which was to become the main test centre for the TSR-2, and supersonic speed was investigated en route for the first time:

British Aircraft Corporation (Operating) Ltd
Preston Division
Experimental Flight Report No. 14

Date:	22 February 1965
Aircraft type:	TSR.2
serial no.:	XR.219
Object of test:	Cruise performance, supersonic handling, and delivery to BAC Warton.
Pilot:	R. P. Beamont
Navigator:	P. J. Moneypenny

Take-off loading

Fuel (indicated contents)	
Forward group:	11,800 lb
No. 2 tank:	4200 lb
Aft group:	9300 lb
No. 4 tank:	3400 lb
Total ind. fuel:	21,100 lb
Fuel	
usable:	21,651 lb
unusable:	1687 lb
total:	23,338 lb
Tare weight and equipment:	58,371 lb
Crew:	340 lb
LOX:	24 lb
Total take-off weight:	82,073 lb

XR219 climbing towards Wallasey TACAN beacon for the start of its first supersonic test, heading north-west over the Irish Sea on flight 14, February 1965. *(British Aerospace)*

Flight no.:	14
Take-off time:	13.13 hr
Landing time:	13.56 hr
Total flight time:	0.43 hr
Time from start-up to shut-down:	1.17 hr
CG position at take-off:	22.2 in AOD (40.1 per cent SMC, U/C extended)

Engines

type:	Bristol Olympus 320X
serial no. 1:	22210
serial no. 2:	22215

Pre-flight checks completed to Flight Reference Cards Issue 3, amended 10 February 1965. Time from entry to completion of checks and engine starts, approximately fifteen minutes.

Fuel: F. 11900/A. 9200 lb

C.G:	G. 39.5 per cent F. 39.5 per cent
Undercarriage indicator:	Nose red, three greens
Aileron gearing indicator:	Ten degrees
Altimeter zeros:	Standby 1013 mb
	Main 1011 mb
Brake accumulators:	3200/3000 psi
Brakes:	F. 1500/1550 psi
	A. 1500/1500 psi
Compass heading checks:	076/076 degrees
Auxiliary intake doors:	Open/Open
Oxygen:	Full/130 psi
Lower aerial:	Selected
ADC Check:	1. 6500 ft
	2. 45,450 ft

Engine Starts

No. 1	
T5:	12.5 sec
30 per cent:	35 sec
Idle:	59.5 per cent/304°C
No. 2	
T5:	14 sec
30 per cent:	31 sec
Idle:	57.8 per cent/294°C
Undercarriage indicator:	Three greens
Aileron gearing indicator:	Five degrees
Brake accumulators:	4100/4000 psi

While taxying at 60/60 per cent an aft fuel transfer was noted with the CG at G moving from 39.2 to 39.5 in a period of approximately 8 minutes with a loss of fuel differential of 700 lb.

The aircraft was stopped on the run-up point and power increased to 70/70 per cent N_h, and then to 90/90 per cent for nozzle over-ride and flap checks, after transferring to bring the fuel back into 2500 lb balance differential and the CG Gauge to 39.2.

Nozzle override checks:	Shut/Shut
Flap blow checks	
Flaps 20°:	Blow in mid-20° segment
Flaps 35°:	Blow in mid-35° segment
Flaps 50°:	blow in mid-35° segment
CG checked after reducing	
to 70/70 per cent:	G. 39.2, F. 39.3

After discussion with the Flight Test Van it was decided to accept this out-of-balance case as probably transitory.

Heading checks:	168°/168°
Max. Dry Normal:	98.4/97.7 per cent, 726/706°C

Reheat lights and staging to third gutter satisfactory, and take-off normal with lift-off at approximately 190 kt, Runway 06, wind 080°/5 kt.

'Double Datum Intermediate' selected immediately after take-off and followed by undercarriage 'UP' selection at approximately 210 kt.

The climb angle was maintained to hold speed below 220 kt during the undercarriage cycle which was normal, and cloud was entered at 1,700 ft before completion of the undercarriage light sequence.

Reheat was cancelled passing 4,000 ft, and the cloud layer cleared at 5,500 ft/ 300 kt at 96.2/96.0 per cent N_h (Max. Dry Intermediate). Flaps twenty degrees to zero at 260 kt after nearly forgetting them.

Speed was slowly increased on the climb heading (351 degrees) to 350 kt/0.8 IMN, at 17,000 ft where a small amount of left rudder trim was required to centre the slip ball and correct a light asymmetric lateral stick force. Use of the rudder trimmer was more coarse than the pitch and roll trim circuits, and tended to result in over-correction.

On the northerly climb heading, reception with Southern Radar and with Boscombe Radar was soon reduced to 'Strength 2' (lower aerial), and Warton Radar was received 5/5 from 20,000 ft at approximately 150 nm.

Boscombe TACAN was held on back bearing as far as Wallasey, where Middleton was selected with Warton Offset and lock-on achieved.
25,000 ft/0.86 IMN.   95/95 per cent.   666/640°C.

All systems serviceable and flight conditions comfortable except for the cabin conditioning. This had been set at 'Normal' for take-off and after ten minutes had resulted in cold conditions in the pilot's cockpit, and uncomfortably cold in the navigator's. 'Auto Full Warm' was selected for the next ten minutes, but this failed to change the temperature which remained uncomfortably cold. In an attempt to prove the sense action of the selector, it was moved back to '⅓rd' from 'Full Cold' and after five minutes no temperature change was noted, so it was re-set at 'Normal' for the rest of the flight; the temperature in the pilot's cockpit becoming a little warmer during the subsequent descent, but the navigator's remained uncomfortably cold throughout.

Speed was increased to 0.9 IMN/25,000 ft and level flight established at 0.92/ 28,000 ft, power reduced to 82/82 per cent initially. At 0.9 IMN the chase Lightning reported 0.89/344 kt.

During the climb pitch control and damping were excellent as was the directional case, and above 20,000 ft the lateral control became noticeably lighter but still adequately damped. In the level cruise the effects of inertia in the roll axis were noticeable with sharp inputs, but not with normally smooth stick movements.

Heading holding was of a high standard, and in this first experience constant attention was not given to steering accuracy due to preoccupation with other observations. In spite of this whenever the Heading Indicator was referred to, it was found to be within a degree or so of the originally selected heading throughout the twenty-minute cruise. This same effect was apparent subsequently when setting up recovery headings for instrument descent, when heading holding accuracy was of a high order and required little concentration.

Altimeter checks on Boscombe QFE (1013 mb)
Standby: 29,000 ft
Main: 29,100
0.92 IMN.:   86/86 per cent

While preoccupied with taking observations, maintaining height was not as easy as at lower altitudes and a steady drift up occurred.

In one speed excursion IMN was allowed to reach 0.935 when mild buffet vibration was felt. For the rest of the cruise approximately 0.92 was maintained at 84/85 per cent NH, 450/488°C T5.

It was noted, that the small power corrections necessary to stabilise speed were difficult to set up with this throttle control in the 85 per cent N_h range. Engine control was more precise above 90 per cent.

At Wallasey it was decided to use the Test Run 'A' supersonic run under Warton control, monitored by Ulster; position monitored by Middleton TACAN with Warton Offset. Power was increased to 'Max. Dry Intermediate' giving 95/95 per cent N_h, and as IMN increased, mild buffet vibration began at 0.93/30,000 ft and reduced on passing 0.98 until no vibration was present at Mach 1.

No perceptible trim changes had occurred in this acceleration, and lateral damping had increased until the sensation of lightness/inertia in the lateral control had disappeared.

P3 indication on the port engine was virtually off the bottom end of the scale at approximately fifty to sixty psi. This was outside the scheduled limits for reheat light. The condition was discussed with Warton Flight Test, who confirmed that this could be a gauge error and suggested a cautious investigation of reheat ignition within the prescribed limiting height/speed channel.

While the discussion was in progress some unsteadiness was noted in ASI and Altimeter, and at 1.0/400 kt the jump-up occurred to 1.01/405 kt with Main Altimeter jump-up amount not recorded accurately. This condition occurred in a slight descent from 30,500, and the aircraft was levelled out again at 30,000 ft with jump-up/jump-down indications continuing spasmodically. There were no associated trim changes or vibrations.

With No. 2 engine maintaining Max. Dry Intermediate, No. 1 reheat was lit satisfactorily and appeared to shunt between one and two gutters. The throttle was moved forward progressively to third cutter which stabilised, and acceleration continued in this condition.

Speed increased quite quickly with a clear jump-up on the altimeter, but less than 5 kt on the ASI, and was continued to 1.12/440 kt/29,500 ft.

Use of No. 1 reheat and third gutter only, resulted in a slight starboard directional trim change (half slip ball), and this was corrected with a small port rudder trim input.

Flight conditions supersonic remained smooth and trim change-free, and damping and response to small inputs on all three axes was smooth and precise. Any tendency towards feeling the effects of inertia in the lateral sense disappearing above Mach 1.

With No. 1 reheat only, fuel asymmetry developed normally and this was contained satisfactorily with the use of the transfer system. (F. 7600/A. 5000 lb.)

The chase aircraft confirmed passing the jump-up condition, but had fallen behind during transition and was not able to give a steady state speed check.

No. 1 reheat was cancelled, and a port turn initiated maintaining height and allowing speed to reduce in the turn at approximately 2 g. The jump-down occurred with no trim change and without buffet onset until slight vibration reappeared at approximately 0.98 IMN. This disappeared again at 1.5 g/0.9 IMN approximately.

With extensive cloud cover and a 5000 ft thick cloud sheet below 6500 ft, a practical instrument descent condition was established during the intitial recovery pattern for a radar controlled cloud break to Warton, monitored by Offset TACAN.

Reducing IMN from 0.9 to 0.8 and subsequently to 370–350 kt, with half airbrake from 15,000 ft and power to trim a 3500 ft per minute descent, resulted in practical and pleasant instrument conditions.

Cloud penetration was made at fixed power (approximately 80/80 per cent) in view of possible icing, and instrument flight in cloud from 6000–1700 ft was steady and conducive to confidence. Scan of the main Head-Down Display was not satisfactory, due to the wide separation of the VSI from the other main references, and it was once again easier to fly on the Standby group alone as this contains the VSI well within normal scan.

The circuit was joined with one-and-a-half miles' visibility in smoke haze, and a low level run carried out from east to west across Warton at 150 ft/460 kt. As before, control conditions in this configuration were smooth and precise, and no disturbance was felt from turbulence. (Fuel: F. 6800/A. 4200 lb.)

A gentle climbing turn was initiated while reducing power, and at approximately 450 kt/2.0–2.5 g, about two seconds of high frequency vibration was felt. This was of low amplitude and approximately 35–40 cps, and disappeared on reducing g, but this may have been coincidental.

Speed was further reduced and the aircraft lined up at 320 kt for a second run, and during the turn the buffet boundary was encountered clearly at 2 g. (Fuel F. 6300/A. 3800 lb.)

The TSR2 landing at Warton at the end of flight 14, with Warton's 'chase' Canberra B2, serial WD937 overhead. *(British Aerospace)*

Speed was reduced to 210 kt, and undercarriage 'DOWN' selected. The cycle appeared normal but left the 'Starboard RED' on (flickering) for two to three minutes. This went out leaving no lights on the starboard leg, and the landing was continued on the basis of visual confirmation of the ankle-lock by periscope and the chase aircraft. (Fuel F. 6200/A. 3700 lb.)

On final approach to 08 runway (approach lights at 2 nms, wind/velocity 055 degrees/7 kt, dry surface) judgement of flare point over the undershoot caravan site was not too easy, but the touchdown occurred at 4.2 ft/sec and was accompanied by undercarriage/airframe lateral oscillation for approximately two seconds at ± 1.5 g/5 cps, approximately. Tail parachute normal. Wheel braking increased to maximum at 100 kt. (Fuel F. 5700/A. 3200 lb.)

The turn to back-track was carried out at the confluence with the eastern perimeter track, and the practical turning radius did not seem suitable for a normal 180 degree turn within the runway width itself, under all operating conditions.

Shut-down checks recorded by Navigator.

Summary
In cruise conditions at 30,000 ft the cabin conditioning system temperature control was unsatisfactory, and the cockpits became uncomfortably cold.

Stability and control (un-auto-stabilised) over the currently explored flight envelope from 160–520 kt at low level, and to 1.1 IMN/30,000 ft is of a high quality and requires no design action.

Speed stability and control of the cruise condition at 0.9/30,000 ft is similar to other aircraft in this category; but the transition characteristics, which lack buffet or trim change, are superior to those of any other aircraft flown by the writer.

The transition jump-up was reached unexpectedly at 'Max. Dry Intermediate' in a slight descent at 30,000 ft (Met. temperature: $-52°C$).

The first reheat light-up at altitude was satisfactory. In the first full instrument recovery on this aircraft, instrument platform characteristics proved favourable as predicted. Some unsatisfactory features were confirmed in the Head-Down Display layout.

At Warton, the test sortie rate increased sharply, and in a total of twenty-four flights a remarkably high rate of test achievement was demonstrated before the programme was cancelled abruptly in the Budget Speech of 6 April 1965.

Prior to that, BAC had been able to produce detailed evidence that the TSR.2 had demonstrated, beyond any reasonable doubt, that it was a most successful aeroplane and basically well able to achieve the complex tasks required of it.

At the time *Flight International* commented:

This weapons system is far more than just a replacement for the Canberra. It is likely to prove the only one of its generation able to hit the enemy bridge, and the correct span of the bridge, after a deep penetration of any type of enemy defences.

It will provide the Royal Air Force with a full range of options to react effectively and economically to any military situation anywhere.

Application of a Pentagon-style cost effectiveness study to TSR.2 and all available alternatives, drives home the fact that this new, all-British aircraft is one item of equipment we cannot afford not to have.

This terrain-following, high speed, multi-role, strike and reconnaissance concept, and the reality of the successful design and build programme, and of the flight testing as

Warton's unique lineage: The Mach 2.5 TSR2, the Mach 2.2 Lightning Mk. 6 and the 50,000 feet
Canberra Mk. B2, photographed together after the cancellation of TSR2 in Spring 1965. *(British Aerospace)*

far as it was allowed to go, had by 1965 established BAC in the vanguard of world
technology in this field. There was no other programme in existence to challenge it;
the nearest rival being the F-111 development programme which, though similar in
military role capability, was less capable in many aspects of performance than the
TSR.2.

The F-111 eventually did have one significant advantage however — it was not
cancelled, and it survived to provide the USAF with a unique strike capability
unrivalled until the arrival of the Tornado.

In the 1970s and '80s, but for the challenge and stimulus of the TSR.2, the
technology vitally needed for the Tornado and EFA might well have been
unavailable in this country.

In its short life the TSR.2 proved to have the remarkable qualities of control and
stability essential for its demanding roles at extremely low altitudes and high speeds.
It was shown, in fact, to be a major technical success and was set fair to provide the
RAF with a quantum stride forward in both tactical and strategic capabilities.

Twenty-five years later, the least that can be said is that the TSR.2 had
demonstrated once again the formidable potential of Britain's aviation industry in
the demanding field of aviation technology.

Chapter Seven
Conclusion

By 1965 the scene was set for the remaining years of the century. Military aviation would move forward from practical transonic to highly supersonic speeds which, in the absence of the problems of control and stability of the 'compressibility' period, would be limited only by very high rates of fuel consumption (and cost), and by the effects of thermal stress beyond Mach 2.

As a result of military experience, civil aviation was already considering the implications of airline operation at Mach 2 to replace the Mach 0.75 cruise of the big jets of the period. Military experience suggested that long range operations at up to

Brian Trubshawe and John Cochrane in the cockpit of the British prototype Concorde prior to its first flight on 9 April 1969. Note the incomplete cockpit instrumentation. *(British Aerospace)*

twice the speed of sound would present no insuperable operational problems or environmental difficulties, if limited to overseas routes where the sonic boom overpressure would not cause disturbance to populations. Supersonic operations overland would be a different matter and could well be banned.

With considerable courage and foresight the British and French Governments set up a joint programme in which the British Aircraft Corporation and Aerospatiale would design a 100-plus-passenger, Mach 2-cruise airliner for, initially, the premium trans-Atlantic routes Paris-New York and London-New York, non-stop.

The evolution of that great aircraft, the Concorde, has been a saga on all counts. In almost all its technical aspects at or beyond the then-current limits of experience and technology, the programme had major and vociferous opponents in both technical and political spheres, and there were many moments during the ten years from contract date to first flight when it seemed that the detractors would win and the aircraft would never fly.

Nevertheless, on 2 March 1969 at Toulouse, André Turcat and his crew flew 001, the first Concorde, successfully for the first time; and shortly afterwards Brian Trubshaw and John Cochrane flew the second prototype, 002, equally successfully out of Filton to land at Fairford on 9 April 1969.

This was the commencement of another saga of courage, determination and technical achievement of the highest order, for Concorde broke the mould of conventional 1960s jet airliner design (when all long-range airliners were operating at, or close to the tropopause at cruise speeds from Mach 0.75–0.78). It was designed to cruise at Mach 2, between 55–60,000 ft over 3–4000-mile sectors, with international

The North American X15, last in the very successful American series of rock-powered supersonic research aircraft and the fastest conventional aircraft in the world, it exceeded Mach 6, 4,500 mph and 360,000 feet during its test programme from 1959-68. *(John W. R. Taylor)*

The SR-71A triple-sonic reconnaissance aircraft. *(John W. R. Taylor)*

standard diversion fuel margins and conventional passenger safety and comfort standards.

Concorde's performance was significantly in excess of any large military aircraft of its day; the nearest contender in speed over distance being the remarkable Mach 3 Lockheed SR-71 'Blackbird' reconnaissance aircraft, which carried only a crew of two.

The flight trials history of the Concorde when published by test pilot Brian Trubshaw will make remarkable reading, covering so many major advances in aviation at one step; for example, it was the first delta wing, supersonic airliner, the first designed for sustained cruise at twice the speed of sound, and the first to cruise as high as 60,000 ft (20,000 ft above the highest normal cruise altitudes of the subsonic airliner fleet). It was also the first non-military aircraft to cruise at supersonic speed, and the first built to withstand the high dynamic pressures of flight beyond 500 kt indicated airspeed.

In the late 1960s, America (which had attempted and failed to produce a supersonic airliner), banned entry of the potentially successful French and British Concordes into New York — the vital port of entry if the Concorde was to succeed and sell to the other airlines which had reserved provisional delivery slots on the production line. It was banned on spurious environmental grounds for just long enough to ensure cancellation by the other customers and the inevitable cessation of production after completion of the British Airways and Air France orders, with no other orders in sight.

When the potential supersonic competition on the Atlantic was seen to be reduced to only two airlines with a total of fifteen 100-passenger aircraft, the US authorities suddenly found that Concorde's noise levels were, after all, acceptable! The New York ban was lifted and Concorde was allowed to begin the world's first regular supersonic airline service, crossing the Atlantic in three-and-a-half to four hours with a reliability which has become legendary in its first ten years of operation.

In those ten years, Americans have been, by a large margin, the predominant users of a service which has brought the two major capitals of Europe to within four hours of New York and Washington.

The resulting major lead in technology has been a source of frustration in the great American aviation industry where, at the time of writing in 1989, major research and 'viability study' programmes were continuing for a second-generation, supersonic airliner. However, it can already be seen that with a mid-life engineering update being planned for 1989, the Concorde fleet will complete its planned twenty years' service and be retired before any replacement becomes available. So that in the year 1999, after twenty years of successful supersonics, the airline world will most probably return to subsonic performance (ie, less than half the speed of Concorde), at least for some years.

However, despite this period of frustration, American aviation and space technology made one of the most significant advances of all — the achievement of orbital space flight and hypersonic atmosphere recovery to an almost conventionally controlled runway landing by a passenger- and freight-carrying airliner-sized aircraft — the Space Shuttle.

Minutes after re-entry from Earth orbit, Space Shuttle Columbia enters the final phase of its steep 'energy-management' glide approach over the Mojave desert towards its landing at Edwards Air Force Base, California. *(Taylor Photo Library)*

15 May 1989 was, for the author, a day of great professional interest and pride in British and European aviation achievement, and also some nostalgia. It had been twenty-one years since I had last flown at Mach 2. Now I was to fly to Washington and Miami in the British Airways Concorde, observing much of it from the flight deck. At 16.30 hr GMT, Captain Boas opened the throttles of Concorde no. 14 G-BOAG, on London Heathrow's Runway 28 Left (take-off weight 155,000 kg), stabilised maximum dry power briefly to check all engine parameters and released the brakes. The auto throttle system then selected reheat on all four Olympus engines, as Concorde reached 80 kt.

To the author, Concorde's acceleration was reminiscent of though not as quick as a Lightning fighter: 190 kt, nosewheel lift, came up at +28 seconds; 'rotation' continued to lift-off at 210 kt at +38 seconds; undercarriage retraction with little disturbance; and then the difference — power reduced with reheat cancellation at 250 kt for the standard noise abatement procedure, while the INS (inertial navigation system) settled the autopilot on to the first heading for the route, London-Washington.

On breaking ground, airframe roughness had been apparent which did not clear as the undercarriage retracted smoothly. This mild buffet resulted from the leading-edge vortex pattern swirling across the deep-chord delta wing in a 250-kt, high angle-of-attack (the angle of incidence of the wing to the airflow), noise abatement climb, which was maintained until passing 5000 ft west of Newbury.

The vapour pattern of the wing vortex could be seen clearly from the cabin windows, spreading from the leading edge close in to the fuselage. This condition was elimated as AoA reduced with speed increase above 290 kt after six minutes ten seconds from take-off.

The windscreen visor had been raised four minutes after take-off, eliminating all noisy airflow roughness as Concorde settled into its smooth initial subsonic climb sector heading for the west-bound, supersonic acceleration point over the Bristol Channel.

Concorde in supersonic cruise configuration with visor 'up'. *(British Aerospace)*

Subsonic climb sector

SPEED	HEIGHT	TEMP.	TIME SINCE TAKE-OFF
Mach .88	20,000 ft	−24°C	10 mins 10 secs
Mach .90	22,300 ft	−24°C	10 mins 40 secs
Mach .94	24,500 ft	−24°C	11 mins 30 secs
Mach .95	26,000 ft	−37°C	11 mins 45 secs
Mach 1	28,000 ft	−42°C	17 mins 55 secs

Transition to supersonic was imperceptible and reheats were re-lit again in pairs (giving only slight longitudinal 'nudges'), to continue accelerating in the climb.

SPEED	HEIGHT	TEMP.	TIME SINCE TAKE-OFF
Mach 1.5	39,500 ft		24 mins 20 secs
Mach 1.65	42,000 ft	−58°C	26 mins (1000 mph (T))
Mach 1.8	45,000 ft	−57°C	29 mins 25 secs
(Minor clear-air turbulence — seatbelts sign 'ON' passing 45,000 ft)			
Mach 1.9	47,000 ft	−55°C	34 mins 56 secs

As the outside air temperature inversion rose eventually to − 53°C at 49,000 ft, the climb levelled and the Concorde continued to accelerate to its economic cruise point of Mach 2 at 49–50,000 ft for eighteen minutes until encountering colder air again. On reaching the cruise point, the auto-throttle system cancelled the reheats.

Passing through 50,000 ft, the main ocean cruise sector began with the engines continuing at 'max dry' (ie, without reheat); with the Machmeter steady at 2.0 and altitude slowly increasing in the 'cruise-climb' as the fuel burn reduced the total weight.

This constant Mach number/constant IAS cruise-climb technique was a repeat of the much earlier standard jet procedure, established first by the English Electric Canberra in 1949 at the beginning of the long-range jet era. In those days the cruise speed over long sectors was from Mach 0.72–0.75 between 40–48,000 ft; now, in 1989, it was at continuous Mach 2 from 55–60,000 ft — a mammoth advance in a mere forty years.

However, from the military pilot's point of view the advance was not quite so staggering. Concorde's Mach 2 cruise at close to the 530-kt indicated airspeed limit, is modest in comparison with the 700-kt (IAS) clearance of the Lightning and F-104, way back in 1958, and the 800 kt of the TSR.2 and the later Century-series fighters of the 1960s; and, of course, the Tornado of the 1980s. So that, in terms of high dynamic pressure, Concorde, though more than twice as fast as all other jet airliners, is still a moderate and conventional aeroplane in the structural sense; the 530-kt 'Q' limit comparing with the 500-kt limit cleared for the Canberra in 1949.

Where Concorde has always been unique, and will remain so for years to come, is in its capability of sustained cruise over three-to-four-hour sectors at twice the speed of sound — an ability which no other aircraft in the world can match without in-flight refuelling.

The cruise/climb continued:

SPEED	HEIGHT	TEMP.	TIME SINCE TAKE-OFF
Mach 1.96	48,000 ft	−53°C	44 mins 20 secs (1250 mph (T))
Mach 2	49,500 ft	−53°C	45 mins 20 secs
(550 nm west of Land's End, with 3160 nm to go to Washington).			

Throughout this phase there had been total cloud cover below, brilliantly reflecting the sun's glare in contrast to the deep blue of the sky above the hard-rimmed horizon which, at this height, was 300 nm distant.

In the passenger cabin the outside glare was not reflected strongly by the dove-grey upholstery which, together with a light grey cloth above the line of the small windows, gave a restful appearance to the interior; and the only features distinguishing this aircraft from conventional airliners were the noticeable (but not uncomfortable) heat radiation through the windows resulting from the outer skin temperature in the Mach-2 cruise of 100+°C, and the exceptionally comfortable leather-covered seats.

An hour-and-a-quarter after take-off the British Airways cabin staff were serving lunch (immaculate by any standards and remarkable for airline travel) with pleasant efficiency, given the restricted space, and in smooth, steady flight, with all clear-air turbulence well behind and below as the cruise climb resumed in colder air. The passengers would finish their lunch in comfort as the Concorde began its deceleration and descent south east of Newfoundland.

In the meantime the Concorde continued its supersonic, cruise-climb:

SPEED	HEIGHT	TEMP.	TIME SINCE TAKE-OFF
Mach 2	49,500 ft	−53°C	1 hr 15 mins (1300 mph (T))
Mach 2	50,500 ft	−54°C	1 hr 20 mins (2600 nm to go)
Mach 2	52,500 ft	−56°C	1 hr 33 mins
Mach 2	54,500 ft	−59°C	1 hr 54 mins
Mach 2.01	58,000 ft	−61°C	2 hrs 40 mins (Top of climb)

The Concorde was now over the mid-Atlantic, cruising smoothly at twice the speed of sound at close to 60,000 ft (approximately 20,000 ft higher than any other airliner then-current in the world); with the comfortable certainty that there could be absolutely no other civil traffic until descending into the congested, conventional New York/Washington control zones. Also there were very few military aircraft that could operate at this combination of speed and altitude, and none that could do so over mid-Atlantic without in-flight refuelling.

On the flight deck the crew were already busy anticipating the soon-to-be-commenced descent and approach procedures into the New York and Washington air traffic control zones. Meanwhile the passengers were midway through their enjoyable and beautifully served meals, travelling faster than the sun eleven miles high.

The X15, the world's fastest aircraft launching from its B52 mothership.

The X15 landing on one of the salt-lake runways in the Californian Mojave desert.

With Newfoundland clear on the radar to starboard, the deceleration point was approaching:

SPEED	HEIGHT	TEMP.	TIME SINCE TAKE-OFF
Mach 2	57,000 ft	−61°C	2 hrs 59 mins (1290 mph (T) 770 nm to go)
Mach 2	57,000 ft		3 hrs 08 mins

Descent began at 470 kt IAS, increasing to the Q limit 530 KIAS passing 54,000 ft, still at Mach 2.

At three hours and twelve minutes since take-off, the Concorde descended through 45,000 ft at Mach 1.5; then through Mach 1 to subsonic, eighty miles off Cape Cod.

With overcast still solid below, deceleration was continued to subsonic at 40,000 ft; and then down to pattern speed 260 kt, at 10,000 ft, 3.20 hr after take-off. At that point the wing vortex roughness reappeared, and the noise level increased as the visor was lowered to the landing position.

Due to low cloud and rain at Washington/Dulles a short traffic delay occurred, and then the undercarriage was lowered three hours and twenty-nine minutes after take-off as the Concorde turned onto its steady final approach, nose-high, and again with long visible vortices trailing in the damp atmosphere from the wing leading edges.

Touchdown at 150 KIAS occurred at 20.34 hrs (BST), four hours after take-off from London. It had been a remarkable experience of the advances already made (and to be expected in the future), in travel speed and comfort — but then, the let-down! Passenger handling in what should have been a short, comfortable turn-round prior to the Miami sector, was prolonged and extremely uncomfortable due to the Dulles airport passenger handling department; and more of this was to occur in the next sector.

I flew the whole Washington-Miami sector in Concorde No. 14 on the flight deck and, viewed from the 'check' seat behind the captain and immediately alongside the flight engineer, this was an interesting operation.

Despite the long nose forward of the nosewheel, motion on the flight deck while taxiing was subdued and much less than that on many large aircraft, and through the narrow two-main-panels windscreen the view forward was more like that in a military aircraft.

With brakes off at 21.45 hr (BST), stopwatch zero, the second take-off seemed to be more leisurely than it had done in the passenger cabin; and again the numbers showed that, although at a low take-off weight for the short sector, the performance was still less dramatic than in, for example, the Lightning mach 2+ fighter, only recently retired from the RAF after twenty-eight years' good service.

The take-off drill was unchanged: Lift off at 210 kt, 30 seconds (Lightning 14.5 sec at 170 kt); noise abatement climb at 250 kt commenced fifty-eight seconds after take-off; visor up at 10,000 ft, 320 kt, 6.55 min.

Subsonic climb and cruise overland to Norfolk, Virginia:

SPEED	HEIGHT	TIME SINCE TAKE-OFF
Mach .85	20,000 ft	13 mins 30 secs
Mach .96	30,000 ft	15 mins 15 secs

Level cruise commenced at 30,000 ft/Mach .95.

Large cumulonimbus visible ahead at 80 nm (radar).

In this phase it was noted that vision sideways through the cockpit side panels was excellent. However, vision forward through the long visor was considerably restricted by the five fore/aft frame parts of the high speed visor itself; by the thick, centre pillar of the main, twin-panelled inner (slow-speed) windscreen; and also by the many bus-bar elements of the Triplex Gold film demisting panels around the edges of the visor panels.

The result (though much improved on the original faulted design concept of a 'solid' forward visor which actually flew on the prototype before being ruled unacceptable by airline aircrew), was still scarcely sufficient to enable comfortable scanning for possible conflicting traffic — still an important requirement, especially in the climb and decent phases.

Clear-air turbulence in the climb through 31–35,000 ft produced only moderate accelerations on the flight deck.

After coasting out at Norfolk, Virginia, reheat acceleration was commenced, level, at 39,000 ft, 42 minutes and 30 seconds after take-off.

Autopilot = 'ATT/HOLD' and 'INS'

Fuel transferred back to fin in anticipation of the nosedown trim change as the centre of pressure moved aft in transition through Mach 1.

Transition:

SPEED	HEIGHT	TIME SINCE TAKE-OFF
Mach 1.01	39,000 ft	43 min (reheat lit in pairs)

Climbing:

SPEED	HEIGHT	TIME SINCE TAKE-OFF
Mach 1.39	42,000 ft	55 mins 20 secs

Air intake ramps moved down to slow down the incoming air to subsonic (monitored on four ramp position gauges on the engineer's panel).

Climbing:

SPEED	HEIGHT	TIME SINCE TAKE-OFF
Mach 1.5	45,000 ft	56 mins 30 secs
Mach 1.74	45,500 ft	57 mins 45 secs (reheats cancelled to 50% fuel burn)
Mach 1.9	48,000 ft	59 mins 40 secs (mild clear air turbulence to 51,000 ft)

Elevons trimmed to zero drag by fin fuel transfer.

Climbing:

SPEED	HEIGHT	TIME SINCE TAKE-OFF
Mach 2	51,000 ft	1 hr 25 mins (525 KIAS/Q max — VNe = 530)
Mach 2.02	55,000 ft	1 hr 4 mins (temp −64°C)
Mach 2	59,000 ft	1 hr 6 mins (top of climb)
Mach 2	59,200 ft	1 hr 8 mins (deceleration begun)
Transition to subsonic, 40,000 ft, 1 hr 17 mins since take-off.		

The approach to Miami was made through rain cloud, with visibility reduced below cloud in heavy showers; with auto throttle and 'ATT/HOLD', 'IAS/ACQ' and 'TRK/HDG' on the autopilot.

Visor down at 1 hour 15 minutes with increased noise level and much improved vision. Under dark cloud the under-shroud lighting of the full instrument panel was even and of excellent quality.

At seven miles final approach, 1700 ft, 192 kt, the wing vortex was causing strong buffeting. Aircraft in manual control from right seat.

HEIGHT	SPEED	TIME SINCE TAKE-OFF
800 ft	184 kt	—
300 ft	150 kt	—
Touchdown	145 kt	1 hr 24 mins

Concorde in subsonic traffic pattern configuration with windscreen visor 'down'. *(British Aerospace)*

This short but superbly flown sector by the world's only supersonic airliner was then followed by over one hour of confusion in handling the passengers through customs and immigration at Miami International airport.

In this operation of a superb aircraft by the world's most professional airline organisation, the London to Miami route had been covered in five hours and twenty minutes' flying time; but the total time for the passengers from departure at London to cleared-customs at Miami was seven hours and thirty minutes. The flight operation could scarcely be improved upon, but it seemed that ground management at Washington Dulles and Miami International airports had clearly yet to arrive in the supersonic era!

But in fairness it must be recorded that on the return flights one week later the passenger handling arrangements at both airports were excellent.

The British and French Concorde Flights carried out their operations with understated, cool efficiency and pride, in the sure knowledge that their job is unique in the world of aviation. There is no other supersonic airliner, nor will there be in the positively predictable future. Concorde and its Atlantic operation are supreme examples of the proven ability of European aviation to lead the world.

Though slow to start, the supersonic age has arrived.

The years 1938-1988, the fifty most eventful years in aviation encompassing the introduction of the first 300 mph multi-gun fighters; the first 200+ mph bombers and airliners; the greatest air war in history; the first jet aircraft; the first supersonic aircraft, and the first capable of twice the speed of sound; the first and only successful supersonic airliner; and the ultimate achievement — space flight with the first atmosphere-recoverable and runway-landing space-plane.

Britain's contribution throughout this era has been of world-leader quality, except for the inexplicable decisions by Parliament to opt out of supersonics in 1947 and, in 1988, to finally opt out of space.

The Hurricane, Spitfire, Lancaster, Mosquito, Typhoon, Tempest, Canberra, Hunter, Victor, Vulcan, Comet, Viscount, VC.10, P.1, FD.2 and Lightning, were all superb aircraft in their time, without superiors anywhere in the world; as are the Harrier, Tornado and Concorde, in 1989.

In addition, many of the brilliant designs which suffered political cancellation in the three decades following World War II had enormous potential; and some had actually reached the point of demonstrating clear technical success when the political axe fell; perhaps the worst example being the BAC TSR.2 supersonic strike aircraft of 1964/65.

The policies of stop-go-stop, specification, procurement, and then cancellation before production, have bedevilled British aviation since World War II; and a new enlightened approach and change in outlook were sadly lacking when, in 1988, the Government announced the withdrawal of support for Britain's only major space programme, Hotol.

This very advanced project was for a commercially viable, aerodynamically launched and recoverable space vehicle, incorporating a breakthrough design of a combined air-breathing and rocket propulsion engine.

During this long period of continuous advance in aviation technology, and massive

The English Electric Lightning 2nd Prototype in 1957. *(British Aerospace)*

sustained effort by British industry, successive governments have failed repeatedly to support the full potential of British achievements in this sphere. Even more importantly, they have failed to understand the inevitable knock-on effects in the wider field of British exports of the British government's implied lack of confidence in British industry, whenever they cancel a major aviation programme.

Fortunately such restraints have not always prevented export success as evidenced by the truly massive Saudi-Arabian export programme won by the British Aircraft Corporation in 1965 against world competition, with the English Electric Lightning. A programme renewed for the third time in 1988 with a massive re-order for Tornados and Hawks, together with training and support worth many thousands of millions of pounds, and ensuring the continued employment of thousands of personnel; it is already a thirty year-plus commitment, which three times consecutively has been acknowledged as the largest single export programme recorded in Britain.

Aviation is recognised as the spearhead of industrial technology, and Britain has demonstrated time and again that it can be a world leader in this field. But this full potential will never be realised until Britain has a government containing politicians trained to understand, and if necessary criticise with sound argument, the specialist advice they receive from the Procurement Executive; and politicians aware of the full implications of the judgements and decisions which they will make on Britain's behalf in this vitally important field.

Bibliography

Supersonic. Richard Hallion, published by Smithsonian Institution.
The Hub. Roger A. Freeman, published by Airlife.
Flying Concorde. Brian Calvert, published by Airlife.
Aeroplane Monthly Magazine

Index